THE

DAILY SPARK

Shakespeare

This edition published by Spark Publishing.

Spark Publishing
A Division of SparkNotes LLC
120 Fifth Avenue, 8th Floor
New York, NY 10011

ISBN 1-4114-0229-4

Please submit changes or report errors to *www.sparknotes.com/errors*.

Written by Emma Chastain.

Printed and bound in the United States.

A Barnes & Noble Publication

Contents

Introduction

The *Daily Spark* series gives teachers an easy way to transform downtime into productive time. The 180 exercises—one for each day of the school year—will take students five to ten minutes to complete and can be used at the beginning of class, in the few moments before turning to a new subject, or at the end of class. A full answer key in the back of the book provides detailed explanations of each problem.

The exercises in this book may be photocopied and handed out to the class, projected as a transparency, or even read aloud. In addition to class time use, they can be assigned as homework exercises or extra credit problems.

Shakespeare can be intimidating, but the *Shakespeare Daily Spark* is a great way to make his work accessible, relevant, and fun. The exercises tackle the Bard using a variety of methods: They ask students to "translate" key quotations by putting his words into modern English; they encourage students to write dialogue inspired by Shakespeare's dialogue; and they draw students' attention to Shakespeare's bawdy humor and thrilling plots.

Spark your students' interest with the *Shakespeare Daily Spark*!

Shakespeare Coined the Phrase . . .

"budge an inch":

SLY: *I'll not budge an inch, boy; let him come and kindly.*
(falls asleep)

(Induction.i.15)

In *The Taming of the Shrew*, the drunken Christopher Sly speaks this now-common phrase, then immediately passes out. **Use the phrase "budge an inch" in three very short paragraphs of your own, each paragraph spoken by a different character. Make one character furious, one scared, and one brave.**

The Taming of the Shrew

At the beginning of *The Taming of the Shrew*, a lord stumbles across a drunkard, Sly, who has passed out in the street. The lord decides to play a trick on him: he takes the sleeping Sly to a beautiful room in his house and orders his servants to treat Sly like a lord when he wakes up. The servants will pretend that Sly has been suffering from delusions for fifteen years, imagining that he was a common drunk when in fact he was a lord the entire time. A male page employed by the lord dresses up as Sly's wife. When Sly awakens, he is quickly taken in by the trick. He wants to sleep with his "wife" right away. **Put the page's response in your own words, using modern English.**

PAGE: *Thrice noble lord, let me entreat of you*
To pardon me yet for another night or two.
Or if not so, until the sun be set.
For your physicians have expressly charged,
In peril to incur your former malady,
That I should yet absent me from your bed.
(Induction.ii.114–119)

The Taming of the Shrew

The bulk of *The Taming of the Shrew* is a story within a story, a play put on for the amusement of Sly, a vagrant who becomes the object of an elaborate practical joke. In the play, a young nobleman named Lucentio arrives in Padua to study at the university there. His servant, Tranio, gives him a little advice about studying. **Put Tranio's advice in your own words, using modern English.**

TRANIO: *Music and poesy use to quicken you;*
The mathematics and the metaphysics—
Fall to them as you find your stomach serves you.
No profit grows where is no pleasure ta'en.
(I.i.36–39)

The Taming of the Shrew

Katherine Minola, the shrew of the play's title, is the older sister of Bianca. Baptista Minola, the father of Katherine and Bianca, won't let anyone court Bianca until Katherine has been married off. Hortensio, who is in love with Bianca, describes Katherine to Petruchio, who is in search of a rich wife. **Put his description in your own words, using modern English.**

HORTENSIO: *I can, Petruchio, help you to a wife*
With wealth enough, and young and beauteous,
Brought up as best becomes a gentlewoman.
Her only fault, and that is faults enough,
Is that she is intolerable curst,
And shrewd and froward. . . .
(I.ii.82–87)

The Taming of the Shrew

Hortensio, disguised as a music teacher, attempts to instruct Katherine. Read the following passage and then explain in your own words what happened at the music lesson.

HORTENSIO: *I did but tell her she mistook her frets,*
And bowed her hand to teach her fingering,
When, with a most impatient devilish spirit,
"'Frets' call you these?" quoth she. "I'll fume with them!"
And with that word she struck me on the head,
And through the instrument my pate made way
And there I stood amazed for a while
As on a pillory, looking through the lute,
While she did call me "rascal fiddler"
And "twangling Jack"; with twenty such vile terms,
As had she studied to misuse me so.
(II.i.149–159)

The Taming of the Shrew

Petruchio ignores Katherine's insults and vocal expressions of dislike for him, and he forces her to marry him. In a calculated move, he shows up to the church late, wears offensively ugly clothes to the ceremony, and swears at the priest. Then he calls Katherine his property and whisks her away before the reception has even started.

Why do you think he behaves this way? Explain.

The Taming of the Shrew

Petruchio torments Katherine, refusing to let her eat or sleep and pretending all the time that he's doing nothing wrong. One day, they set out for the house of Katherine's father. Petruchio insists the moon is out, even though it is actually daytime. Katherine contradicts him, but when Petruchio threatens to cancel the trip, she gives in and says the moon *is* out.

KATHERINE: *I know it is the moon.*
PETRUCHIO: *Nay, then you lie. It is the blessèd sun.*
KATHERINE: *Then God be blessed, it is the blessèd sun.*
But sun it is not, when you say it is not,
And the moon changes even as your mind.
What you will have it named, even that it is,
And so it shall be so for Katherine.
(IV.v.17–23)

Why is this a crucial turning point in Katherine and Petruchio's marriage? What has Katherine said? Explain.

The Taming of the Shrew

By the end of the play, Petruchio has changed Katherine completely, to the shock of her friends and family. She gives a long speech to other, less obedient wives, urging them to respect their husbands. An excerpt:

KATHERINE: *Thy husband is thy lord, thy life, thy keeper,*
Thy head, thy sovereign, one that cares for thee . . .
when [a wife] is forward, peevish, sullen, sour,
And not obedient to his honest will,
What is she but a foul contending rebel
And graceless traitor to her loving lord?
(V.ii.155–156, 166–169)

Think about your own ideas about how wives should behave. **Then write a speech of your own expressing those ideas.**

The Taming of the Shrew

If you were casting a movie version of *The Taming of the Shrew*, which actors would you pick to play Katherine and Petruchio? Why?

Shakespeare Coined the Phrase . . .

"all the world's a stage":

JAQUES: *All the world's a stage,*
And all the men and women merely players:
They have their exits and their entrances;
And one man in his time plays many parts,
His acts being seven ages.
(II.vii.139–143)

In this passage from *As You Like It,* Jaques says that the world is like a stage, and the people in the world are like actors who enter (are born) and exit (die), passing through several stages of life while they're on stage (alive). Jaques goes on to list the seven stages of life. Do you think your life is like a play, movie or television show? Come up with an idea for a new show based on your own life.

Shakespeare Coined the Phrase . . .

"we have seen better days":

DUKE SENIOR: *True is it that we have seen better days,*
And have with holy bell been knoll'd to church
And sat at good men's feasts and wiped our eyes
Of drops that sacred pity hath engender'd:
And therefore sit you down in gentleness
And take upon command what help we have
That to your wanting may be minister'd.
(II.vii.120–126)

In *As You Like It,* the duke admits that he and his men are down on their luck, but he claims they still have their refined manners. Use the phrase "seen better days" in a two-paragraph story of your own.

Macbeth

Three witches appear in *Macbeth*, casting spells and prophesying Macbeth's fate. In this excerpt, they prepare a spell:

ALL (dancing together in a circle): *The weird sisters, hand in hand,*
Posters of the sea and land,
Thus do go about, about,
Thrice to thine and thrice to mine
And thrice again, to make up nin.
Peace! The charm's wound up.
(I.iii.32–37)

Using these lines as inspiration, write your own witches' chant.

Macbeth

After hearing the witches' prophecy, Macbeth writes to Lady Macbeth, his wife, to tell her that one day he'll be king. Alone, she talks to herself, saying she hopes Macbeth has the guts to do what needs to be done in order to become king—that is, to kill Duncan, the current king. She thinks Macbeth has the ambition, but not the necessary cruel temperament. A messenger arrives to tell Lady Macbeth that her husband is en route to the castle with the king. Lady Macbeth, left alone again, says the king must die. She asks for strength:

LADY MACBETH: *Come, you spirits*
That tend on mortal thoughts, unsex me here,
And fill me from the crown to the toe top-full
Of direst cruelty. Make thick my blood.
Stop up the access and passage to remorse . . .
Come to my woman's breasts,
And take my milk for gall, you murd'ring ministers. . . .
(I.v.41–49)

Analyze this excerpt. What does Lady Macbeth want? Cite specific words and lines from her speech in your answer.

Shakespeare Coined the Phrase . . .

"the be-all and the end-all":

In this passage, Macbeth considers murdering Duncan:

MACBETH: *If it were done when 'tis done, then 'twere well*
It were done quickly. If the assassination
Could trammel up the consequences, and catch
With his surcease success; that but this blow
Might be the be-all and the end-all here,
But here, upon this bank and shoal of time,
We'd jump the life to come.
(I.vii.1–7)

What does Macbeth mean by "the be-all and the end-all"? Explain.

Macbeth

When Macbeth tells his wife he doesn't think he can go through with the plan to kill the king, she accuses him of unmanliness. She says she herself is stronger than Macbeth and would do even the vilest deed if she'd sworn to do it. **Put her speech in your own words, using modern English.**

LADY MACBETH: *I have given suck, and know*
How tender 'tis to love the babe that milks me.
I would, while it was smiling in my face,
Have plucked my nipple from its boneless gums
And dashed the brains out, had I so sworn as you
Have done to this.

(I.vii.54–59)

Shakespeare Coined the Phrase . . .

"the milk of human kindness":

LADY MACBETH: . . . *Yet do I fear thy nature;*
It is too full o' th' milk of human kindness
To catch the nearest way: thou wouldst be great,
Art not without ambition, but without
The illness that should attend it.
(I.v.15–19)

How does Lady Macbeth use the phrase "the milk of human kindness"? How does she characterize her husband? Explain.

Shakespeare Coined the Phrase . . .

"a sorry sight":

Macbeth speaks the words after he has murdered Duncan.

MACBETH (looking at his hands): *This is a sorry sight.*
LADY MACBETH: *A foolish thought, to say a sorry sight.*
(II.ii.18–19)

What do you think Macbeth means by the word *sorry* here? (There are several possibilities.)

Macbeth

After the very somber scene that follows Macbeth's murder of Duncan, Shakespeare gives us a comic interlude in which a drunken porter discusses the three effects of drinking. **What are these three effects? Put the porter's explanation in your own words, using modern English.**

MACDUFF: *What three things does drink especially provoke?*
PORTER: *Marry, sir, nose-painting, sleep, and urine. Lechery, sir, it provokes and unprovokes. It provokes the desire, but it takes away the performance. Therefore, much drink may be said to be an equivocator with lechery. It makes him, and it mars him; it sets him on, and it takes him off; it persuades him, and disheartens him; makes him stand to and not stand to; in conclusion, equivocates him in a sleep, and, giving him the lie, leaves him.*

(II.iii.24–32)

Macbeth

The morning after Duncan's murder, Macduff discovers the corpse and raises the alarm. Lady Macbeth comes running, pretending to be distraught and confused. She asks Macduff to tell her what's going on. He responds:

MACDUFF: *O gentle lady,*
'Tis not for you to hear what I can speak:
The repetition, in a woman's ear,
Would murder as it fell.
(II.iii.78–81)

What is ironic about Macduff's words?

Shakespeare Coined the Phrase . . .

"Knock, knock! Who's there?":

PORTER: *Knock, knock, knock! Who's there? Faith, here's an English tailor come hither for stealing out of a French hose.*

(II.iii.12–13)

In this scene, the porter jokes around by pretending he's standing at the gates of hell and welcoming in a succession of unsavory characters—among them a tailor who skimps on the fabric for his customers' clothes.

Write down three of your favorite knock-knock jokes.

Macbeth

On the night Macbeth murders Duncan, strange occurrences in the natural world mirror the horrifying unnaturalness of Macbeth's deed. It is dark during the daytime, an owl kills a falcon, and Duncan's horses go wild and eat each other.

If you were a writer and wanted to symbolize the horror of an event, what details from the natural world would you write about? List them.

Macbeth

In *Macbeth*, one murder leads to another. Macbeth first kills Duncan; then, perhaps to keep them from talking, he kills the two servants and tries to blame Duncan's murder on them. Even when Macbeth becomes king, he can't relax. He fears Banquo because the witches prophesied that Banquo's descendents would be kings. Macbeth doesn't like to think that the murders he worked hard to commit will help Banquo's sons, so he decides Banquo and his son, Fleance, must be murdered. Macbeth also kills Macduff and Macduff's wife and children.

Suppose you wanted to write a screenplay in which one murder leads to another, as it does in *Macbeth*. Sketch out the plot of this screenplay. Who is the murderer, what is his or her motivation, and what happens?

Macbeth

Even after they've won the kingship they wanted so badly, Macbeth and his wife are unhappy. Lady Macbeth says it's better to be the murdered person than it is to be the killer who must live tormented by anxiety. Macbeth is afflicted by worries and nightmares; "full of scorpions is my mind," he says at one point (III.ii.38).

Take on the voice of either Lady Macbeth or Macbeth and write a description, in the first person, of what you're feeling.

Macbeth

During a dinner party hosted by Macbeth, one of his hired murderers pulls him aside and announces that Banquo has been killed, but Fleance got away. Macbeth returns to the party and is horrified to see a vision of Banquo's ghost sitting at the table. No one else sees the ghost.

LENNOX: *What is't that moves your highness?*
MACBETH: *Which one of you have done this?*
LORDS: *What, my good lord?*
MACBETH (to GHOST): *Thou canst not say I did it. Never shake*
Thy gory locks at me.
ROSS: *Gentlemen, rise. His highness is not well.*
(III.iv.49–54)

Continue your screenplay based on *Macbeth*. Using these lines as inspiration, write a scene in which the murderer addresses the ghost of someone he or she has killed.

The three witches brew a potion in their cauldron, naming the ingredients as they add them:

ALL: *Double, double toil and trouble*
Fire burn, and cauldron bubble.
SECOND WITCH: *Fillet of a fenny snake,*
In the cauldron boil and bake.
Eye of newt and toe of frog
Wool of bat and tongue of dog,
Adder's fork and blind-worm's sting,
Lizard's leg and owlet's wing,
For a charm of powerful trouble,
Like a hell-broth boil and bubble.
(IV.i.10–19)

They also add, among other ingredients, a wolf's tooth, a witch's mummified flesh, a nose, lips, and the finger of a baby that was strangled as its prostitute mother gave birth to it. **What would you include in a heinous witches' brew? If you're feeling ambitious, write the ingredients in rhyming verse form, as Shakespeare does.**

Macbeth

In a heartbreaking scene, Macduff's wife, who feels abandoned by her husband, talks to her young son. Mother and son banter lovingly before a messenger runs in to warn them that they are in danger. Right after the messenger leaves, two thugs come in. The scene ends with affecting simplicity:

FIRST MURDERER (stabbing him): *Young fry of treachery!*
SON: *He has killed me, mother.*
Run away, I pray you!
He dies. Exit LADY MACDUFF, crying "Murder!" followed by MURDERERS.
(IV.ii.80–82)

Write the last lines of a scene of your own, followed by stage directions. Make your lines simple but dramatic, as Shakespeare does.

Macbeth

Ross unwillingly tells Macduff the terrible news: "Your castle is surprised, your wife and babes / Savagely slaughtered" (IV.iii.207–208).

MACDUFF: *My children too?*
ROSS: *Wife, children, servants, all that could be found.*
MACDUFF: *And I must be from thence!*
My wife killed too?
(IV.iii.213–216)

What do Macduff's repeated questions ("My children too?" "My wife killed too?") indicate about his state of mind? Explain.

Shakespeare Coined the Phrase . . .

"one fell swoop":

MACDUFF: . . . *All my pretty ones?*
Did you say all? O hell-kite! All?
What, all my pretty chickens and their dam
At one fell swoop?
(IV.iii.221–224)

In this passage, Macduff likens the murder of his wife and children by Macbeth to the murder of "pretty chickens" by a "hell-kite," a deadly bird of prey. In this context, *fell* means "vicious."

Come up with your own metaphor to describe a vicious act. Try to take your metaphor from the natural world.

Shakespeare Coined the Phrase . . .

"what's done is done":

LADY MACBETH: . . . *Things without all remedy*
Should be without regard: what's done, is done.
(III.ii.11–12)

Write a dialogue in which one person comforts another. End the dialogue with this phrase.

Macbeth

Guilt overtakes Lady Macbeth's mind, and she starts sleepwalking. **Interpret these two excerpts from the scene in which she sleepwalks and talks aloud. To whom is she talking? What do her words mean?**

LADY MACBETH: *Here's the smell of blood still. All the perfumes of Arabia will not sweeten this little hand. Oh, Oh, Oh!*

(V.i.41–42)

LADY MACBETH: *Wash your hands. Put on your nightgown. Look not so pale.—I tell you yet again, Banquo's buried; he cannot come out on's grave.*

(V.i.52–54)

Macbeth

If you were casting a movie version of *Macbeth*, which actors would you pick to play Macbeth and Lady Macbeth? Why?

Macbeth

After he learns that Lady Macbeth has died, Macbeth describes life as "a tale / Told by an idiot, full of sound and fury, signifying nothing" (V.v.27–29).

Think of three fictional characters—characters you've created yourself or characters from books you've read. How would they describe life? Use this frame three times, once for each character:

Life is a tale _____, full of _____, signifying _____.

Shakespeare Coined the Phrase . . .

"eaten me out of house and home":

MISTRESS QUICKLY: *It is more than for some, my lord; it is for all,*
all I have. He hath eaten me out of house and home;
he hath put all my substance into that fat belly of
his: but I will have some of it out again, or I
will ride thee o' nights like the mare.
(II.i.74–78)

In this passage from *Henry IV*, Part 2, Mistress Quickly complains that the obese Falstaff has eaten all of her food, stuffing them "into that fat belly of / his." Describe a particularly rude guest you've hosted at your house. Feel free to include personal insults, as Mistress Quickly does.

Shakespeare Coined the Phrase . . .

"for goodness' sake":

PROLOGUE: *Therefore, for goodness' sake, and as you are known*
The first and happiest hearers of the town,
Be sad, as we would make ye.
(Prologue.23–25)

How does the use of this phrase in Shakespeare's *Henry VIII* differ from our use of it today? Explain.

A Midsummer Night's Dream

Young Hermia is in love with a boy named Lysander, but her father, Egeus, has promised a guy named Demetrius that he can marry Hermia. Although Hermia detests Demetrius, her opinion doesn't matter to her father or to the local government. By law, she must follow her father's wishes, become a nun, or be executed.

Most young people don't face such harsh options, but some parental restrictions on marriage still exist. Do you think your parents would let you marry whomever you wanted? Would they forbid you from marrying anyone based on age, race, occupation, class, or level of education? Write about your parents' attitudes.

Shakespeare Coined the Phrase . . .

"the course of true love never did run smooth":

LYSANDER: *Ay me! For aught I could ever read,*
Could ever hear by tale or history,
The course of true love never did run smooth.
(I.i.132–134)

Judging by your own experience, and that of people you know, do you think Lysander's statement is true? Why or why not?

A Midsummer Night's Dream

Oberon and Titania, king and queen of the fairies, are quarreling over a little boy taken by Titania. Oberon wants to transform him into a knight, but Titania wants to keep him for herself. Over the course of their quarrel, Titania makes an accusation. **Put her speech in your own words, using modern English.**

TITANIA: . . . *I know*
When thou hast stolen away from Fairyland,
And in the shape of Corin sat all day,
Playing on pipes of corn and versing love
To amorous Phillida. Why are thou here,
Come from the farthest step of India?
But that, forsooth, that bouncing Amazon,
Your buskin'd mistress and your warrior love,
To Theseus must be wedded, and you come
To give their bed joy and prosperity.
(II.i.64–73)

A Midsummer Night's Dream

Helena is desperately in love with Demetrius, who loves Hermia. Helena confesses that the worse Demetrius treats her, the more she loves him. She tells him that she is his "spaniel" and begs him, "spurn me, strike me, / Neglect me, lose me" (II. i.204–205).

Do you know people who feel the way Helena does, who can't help but love people who treat them badly? **Write about one such person's attraction to bad boys or bad girls.**

A Midsummer Night's Dream

Oberon knows of a flower that has magical properties: its juice, when rubbed on someone's eyelids, causes that person to fall in love with the first person she sees when she wakes up. Oberon describes the location of the flower in poetic language:

OBERON: *I know a bank where the wild thyme blows,*
Where oxlips and the nodding violet grows,
Quite overcanopied with luscious woodbine,
With sweet musk roses and with eglantine.
There sleeps Titania sometime of the night,
Lulled in these flowers with dances and delight.
And there the snake throws her enameled skin,
Weed wide enough to wrap a fairy in.
(II.i.248–255)

Using lyrical, rhyming language like Oberon's, describe a magical place of your own imagining.

A Midsummer Night's Dream

Oberon squeezes some of the juice from the magic flower onto Titania's eyelids. When she wakes up, the first person she sees is a craftsman named Bottom, whose head has been transformed into that of a donkey by the fairy Puck. Titania falls in love with Bottom, who doesn't seem too surprised by this unlikely development. He points out, "reason and love keep little company together nowadays" (III.i.122–123)—that is, reason and love have very little to do with each other.

Do you agree with Bottom that love is often illogical? Or do you think most people are drawn—logically—to people who resemble them? Explain.

A Midsummer Night's Dream

Bottom and his craftsmen friends prepare a play in honor of Theseus's marriage. They describe it as "'A tedious brief scene of young Pyramus / And his love Thisbe. Very tragical mirth'" (V.i.56–57). After reading this description, Theseus says, "'Merry' and 'tragical'? 'Tedious' and 'brief'? / That is hot ice and wondrous strange snow" (V.i.58–59). **What misuse of language is Theseus pointing out? Explain.**

A Midsummer Night's Dream

At the end of the supposed tragedy, Bottom, who plays Pyramus, stabs himself and makes this speech:

PYRAMUS: *Thus die I, thus, thus, thus.*
Now am I dead.
Now am I fled.
My soul is in the sky.
Tongue, lose thy light.
Moon, take thy flight.
Exit MOONSHINE.
Now die, die, die, die, die.
(dies)
(V.i.286–292)

How are we meant to react to this speech? How do you know?

Shakespeare Coined the Phrase . . .

"good riddance":

PATROCLUS: *No more words, Thersites; peace!*
THERSITES: *I will hold my peace when Achilles' brach bids me, shall I?*
ACHILLES: *There's for you, Patroclus.*
THERSITES: *I will see you hanged, like clotpoles, ere I come any more to your tents: I will keep where there is wit stirring and leave the faction of fools.*
Exit THERSITES.
PATROCLUS: *A good riddance.*
(II.i.108–115)

In this passage from *Troilus and Cressida*, the men exchange harsh words. Thersites suggests that Achilles and Patroclus are homosexual lovers by calling Patroclus "Achilles' brach," which means "Achilles's bitch." Write your own dialogue in which a nasty fight culminates in the phrase "good riddance."

Shakespeare Coined the Phrase . . .

"kill all the lawyers":

CADE: *I thank you good people—there shall be no money. All shall eat and drink on my score, and I will apparel them all in one livery, that they may agree like brothers, and worship me their lord.*
DICK: *The first thing we do, let's kill all the lawyers.*
CADE: *Nay, that I mean to do.*
(IV.ii.71–78)

Why do you think lawyers are hated? Do you think law is the most detested profession today, or does another career field deserve the "most detested" distinction? Explain.

Hamlet

As *Hamlet* opens, King Hamlet has died, and his son, Prince Hamlet of Denmark, mourns him. King Hamlet's wife has quickly married her late husband's brother, Claudius. Hamlet thinks of how much his father loved his mother, and he scorns his mother's new marriage. **Put his angry rant in your own words, using modern English.**

HAMLET: *Why she, even she—*
O God, a beast that wants discourse of reason
Would have mourned longer!—married with my uncle,
My father's brother, but no more like my father
Than I to Hercules.
(I.ii.149–153)

Hamlet

Claudius speaks friendly words to Hamlet, but Hamlet responds with scorn:

CLAUDIUS: *But now, my cousin Hamlet, and my son—*
HAMLET (aside): *A little more than kin and less than kind.*
(I.ii.64–65)

What does the now-famous phrase "more than kin and less than kind" mean?

Hamlet

Many of the most famous phrases from Shakespeare are almost always taken out of context. For instance, the famous mandate "to thine own self be true" is spoken by Polonius, a ludicrous, dim-witted figure who is motivated by self interest (I.iii.78). Polonius is *too* true to himself—he's not loyal to anyone but himself. Moreover, this mandate is one item on a long list of banal advice Polonius gives his son, Laertes.

What is your own opinion of the phrase "to thine own self be true"? Do you think it's good advice, despite the poor character of the person giving the advice in the play? Do you think it's a selfish policy? Explain.

Hamlet

The dead king appears to his son as a ghost and tells him shocking news:

GHOST: *But know, thou noble youth,*
The serpent that did sting thy father's life
Now wears his crown.
(I.v.38–40)

What does the ghost mean by these words?

Hamlet

The ghost explains how he was killed. **Read the following excerpts and then explain, in your own words, what happened.**

GHOST: *Sleeping within my orchard,*
My custom always of the afternoon,
Upon my secure hour thy uncle stole
With juice of cursed hebenon in a vial,
And in the porches of my ears did pour
The leperous distilment . . .
And a most instant tetter barked about,
Most lazar-like, with vile and loathsome crust
All my smooth body.
Thus was I, sleeping, by my brother's hand
Of life, of crown, of queen at once dispatched. . . .
(I.v.59–64, 71–75)

Shakespeare Coined the Phrase . . .

"brevity is the soul of wit":

POLONIUS: *This business is well ended.*
My liege and madam, to expostulate
What majesty should be, what duty is,
Why day is day, night night, and time is time,
Were nothing but to waste night, day, and time.
Therefore, since brevity is the soul of wit,
And tediousness the limbs and outward flourishes,
I will be brief: your noble son is mad:
Mad call I it; for, to define true madness,
What is 't but to be nothing else but mad?
But let that go.

(II.ii.86–96)

What is ironic about Polunius's use of the phrase "brevity is the soul of wit"? Cite specific words and phrases from his speech to back up your statement.

Hamlet

Gertrude and Claudius, fearing that something is wrong with Hamlet, enlist his friends Rosencrantz and Guildenstern to cheer him up. Hamlet, still depressed, asks how Guildenstern came to be trapped in this "prison":

GUILDENSTERN: *Prison, my lord?*
HAMLET: *Denmark's a prison.*
GUILDENSTERN: *Then is the world one.*
HAMLET: *A goodly one, in which there are many confines, wards, and dungeons, Denmark being one o' the worst.*
(II.ii.240–244)

Have you ever felt metaphorically imprisoned? Write about that feeling.

Hamlet

Although the ghost of his father commanded him to seek revenge, Hamlet is paralyzed by indecision. He is outraged about his father's murder, but he finds he "can say nothing" (II.ii.545). He berates himself for his inaction and cowardice:

HAMLET: *Why, what an ass am I! This is most brave,*
That I, the son of a dear father murdered,
Prompted to my revenge by heaven and hell,
Must, like a whore, unpack my heart with words
And fall a-cursing like a very drab,
A scullion!

(II.ii.560–565)

What is Hamlet's tone in this passage? Cite specific words and phrases in your answer.

In a soliloquy that begins, “To be, or not to be” (III.i.57), Hamlet thinks about suicide.

HAMLET: *To sleep, perchance to dream—ay, there’s the rub,*
For in that sleep of death what dreams may come
When we have shuffled off this mortal coil,
Must give us pause.
(III.i.66–69)

Why does death scare us, according to Hamlet? Explain.

Hamlet

Hamlet delivers several celebrated **soliloquies**—speeches delivered alone onstage. In soliloquies, characters think out loud, pouring out their private thoughts. Modern movies and plays don't use soliloquies much, but they do employ similar devices. What are some of these soliloquy-like devices? Write about a few examples of them from movies or plays you've seen recently.

Hamlet

Hamlet goes mad, or at least pretends to go mad—critics have never agreed on whether his madness is real or faked. If Hamlet is faking, he is doing an excellent job: during one conversation with Ophelia, he tells her to go to a convent, says everyone is a criminal, orders her to lock her father inside, and, finally, tells her that wise men understand that women are adulterers.

Imagine you want to convince someone that you've gone insane. Write a mad monologue for yourself.

Shakespeare Coined the Phrase . . .

"piece of work":

HAMLET: *O, reform it altogether. And let those that play your clowns speak no more than is set down for them; for there be of them that will themselves laugh to set on some quantity of barren spectators to laugh too, though in the meantime some necessary question of the play be then to be considered. That's villainous, and shows a most pitiful ambition in the fool that uses it. Go, make you ready.*

Exeunt PLAYERS. Enter POLONIUS, ROSENCRANTZ, and GUILDENSTERN.

HAMLET: *How now, my lord? Will the king hear this piece of work?*

(III.ii.35–42)

What is meant by "piece of work" in this passage? What is meant by the phrase today? Explain.

Hamlet

A group of actors comes to Elsinore, and Hamlet has them put on a play that depicts a man killing his brother by pouring poison in his ear, then marrying his brother's widow. Claudius is furious at this display, and Gertrude is upset. She calls Hamlet to her bedroom. He goes and rages at her, berating her for abandoning her noble first husband for the inferior Claudius. He asks how, at her age, she could give in to lust.

Have you ever cruelly berated your parents or any other authority figures? Perhaps you've only done so in your mind, never aloud. **Write a script in which you tear into an adult as Hamlet tears into his mother.**

Shakespeare Coined the Phrase . . .

"heart of hearts":

HAMLET: . . . *Give me that man*
That is not passion's slave, and I will wear him
In my heart's core, ay, in my heart of heart,
As I do thee.
(III.ii.64–67)

Put this excerpt in your own words, using modern English.

Shakespeare Coined the Phrase . . .

"it smells to heaven":

CLAUDIUS: *Oh, my offense is rank. It smells to heaven.*
It hath the primal eldest curse upon't,
A brother's murder. Pray I can not.
(III.iii.37–39)

Today, this phrase is often modified, as in "it stinks to heaven" or "it stinks to high heaven." Use the original phrase or one of its variations in a paragraph about a current political situation.

Hamlet

If you were casting a movie version of *Hamlet,* which actor would you choose to play Hamlet? Why? (Almost any choice is defensible; Hamlet has been played by everyone from Sarah Bernhardt to Mel Gibson.)

Hamlet

Claudius tells Gertrude that because Hamlet is dangerously insane, he must be sent away to England. Claudius then confronts Hamlet to tell him the news, claiming that this trip is for Hamlet's own good and calling himself Hamlet's loving father. As soon as Hamlet leaves the room, Claudius reveals in a soliloquy that he has ordered the English king to kill Hamlet. **Why do you think Claudius has given this order?**

Hamlet

Hamlet, whose life is now in grave danger, knows he should kill Claudius, as his father commanded him. He tells himself that great men are not those who fight only over truly worthy causes, but those who will fight over a piece of straw if their honor is at stake. While Hamlet has great cause to fight, he seems unable to rouse himself to action.

HAMLET: *How stand I then,*
That have a father killed, a mother stained,
Excitements of my reason and my blood,
And let all sleep[?]
(IV.iv.55–58)

Can you sympathize with Hamlet's indecision, or do you think he has a duty to avenge his father's death immediately? Why or why not?

Polonius dies after Hamlet stabs him, perhaps accidentally; Ophelia goes mad and drowns. Perhaps to provide a little comic relief in the midst of these disasters, Shakespeare gives us a scene featuring two gravediggers. One asks the other a riddle: who is it that builds stronger structures than masons, shipbuilders, and carpenters?

Think of an answer to this riddle. (The gravediggers come up with two.)

Hamlet

An old joke: Two people emerge from a theater after seeing *Hamlet*. One says to the other, "That play was full of famous quotes!" Explain why this joke is (supposed to be) funny.

Shakespeare Coined the Phrase . . .

"the makings of":

THIRD GENTLEMAN: *At length her grace rose, and with modest paces*
Came to the altar; where she kneel'd, and saint-like
Cast her fair eyes to heaven and pray'd devoutly.
Then rose again and bow'd her to the people:
When by the Archbishop of Canterbury
She had all the royal makings of a queen;
As holy oil, Edward Confessor's crown,
The rod, and bird of peace, and all such emblems
Laid nobly on her: which perform'd, the choir,
With all the choicest music of the kingdom,
Together sung 'Te Deum.' So she parted,
And with the same full state paced back again
To York-place, where the feast is held.
(IV.i.82–94)

Use the phrase "the makings of" in three sentences of your own.

Shakespeare Coined the Phrase . . .

"neither rhyme nor reason":

DROMIO OF SYRACUSE: . . . *But I pray, sir, why am I beaten? . . .*
ANTIPHOLUS OF SYRACUSE: *Shall I tell you why?*
DROMIO OF SYRACUSE: *Ay, sir, and wherefore; for they say every why hath a wherefore.*
ANTIPHOLUS OF SYRACUSE: *'Why' first: for flouting me; and then 'wherefore': For urging it the second time to me.*
DROMIO OF SYRACUSE: *Was there ever any man thus beaten out of season, When in the why and the wherefore is neither rhyme nor reason?*
(II.ii.38, 42–48)

In this passage from *The Comedy of Errors*, Dromio complains that he has been beaten up for absolutely no reason. Write a dialogue about a time you were treated unfairly. Make yourself one of the speakers.

The Merchant of Venice

The Merchant of Venice begins in the middle of a conversation:

ANTONIO: *In sooth, I know not why I am so sad.*
It wearies me; you say it wearies you.
But how I caught it, found it, or came by it,
What stuff 'tis made of, whereof it is born,
I am to learn.

(I.i.1–5)

Suppose you wanted to write a play and, like Shakespeare, wanted to begin it in the middle of a conversation. Write the first five lines of your play.

The Merchant of Venice

Put this speech of Gratiano's in your own words, using modern English.

GRATIANO: . . . *Let me play the fool.*
With mirth and laughter let old wrinkles come.
And let my liver rather heat with wine
Than my heart cool with mortifying groans.
(I.i.79–82)

The Merchant of Venice

After talking about his own happy nature, Gratiano criticizes people with gloomy dispositions. **Put his criticism in your own words, using modern English.**

GRATIANO: *There are a sort of men whose visages*
Do cream and mantle like a standing pond,
And do a willful stillness entertain
With purpose to be dressed in an opinion
Of wisdom, gravity, profound conceit,
As who should say, "I am Sir Oracle,
And when I ope my lips, let no dog bark!"
(I.i.88–94)

The Merchant of Venice

Portia, a rich girl, is being courted by men from near and far. Her lady-in-waiting, Nerissa, runs through the list of suitors and asks Portia what she thinks of them. The guy from Naples? Portia says he does "nothing but talk of his horse" and explain how he can shoe a horse himself; she thinks his mother must have had an affair with a blacksmith (I.ii.37–38). Count Palantine? Portia says she'd rather be "married to a death's head with a bone in his mouth" than to him (I.ii.46–47). The German guy? Portia says that if they married and he died, she'd manage to get over it.

Using the conversation between Portia and Nerissa as inspiration, write a dialogue between you and a friend in which you run through a list of people you've dated (or thought about dating) but dismissed for one reason or another. Try to make the dialogue humorous.

The Merchant of Venice

Before he died, Portia's father set up a test: any man who wants to marry his daughter has to choose between three boxes, one gold, one silver, and one lead. Before choosing, he must swear never to marry another woman if he chooses incorrectly and never to tell anyone which box he chose. No one who doesn't deserve Portia's love will choose the right box.

If you fell in love with someone, but you knew that you had to play this box game in order to win him or her—and knew that losing would mean a lifetime of loneliness—would you take the risk and play the game? Why or why not?

The Merchant of Venice

Antonio approaches Shylock, a Jewish moneylender, to ask him for a loan. Shylock responds:

SHYLOCK: *Signor Antonio, many a time and oft*
In the Rialto you have rated me
About my moneys and my usances.
Still have I borne it with a patient shrug,
For sufferance is the badge of all our tribe.
You call me misbeliever, cutthroat dog, . . .
And all for use of that which is mine own.
Well then, it now appears you need my help. . . .
What should I say to you? Should I not say,
"Hath a dog money? Is it possible
A cur can lend three thousand ducats?"
(I.iii.102–107, 108–110, 116–118)

What is Shylock's complaint? What has Antonio done to him, and what does Shylock consider a fair response to Antonio's request for money?

The Merchant of Venice

In one of the most famous deals in literature, Shylock agrees to lend money, interest-free, to Antonio, on one condition:

SHYLOCK: *If you repay me not on such a day,*
In such a place, such sum or sums as are
Expressed in the condition, let the forfeit
Be nominated for an equal pound
Of your fair flesh, to be cut off and taken
In what part of your body pleaseth me.
(I.iii.142–147)

Put Shylock's demand in your own words, using modern English.

The Merchant of Venice

Gratiano says, "All things that are, / Are with more spirit chased than enjoyed" (II.vi.12–13). Do you agree? Do you think the pursuit of something is more exciting than the enjoyment of it once you have it? Explain your feelings on the subject, using examples from your own life.

The Merchant of Venice

The Merchant of Venice is full of nasty slurs against Jews. In a celebrated speech, Shylock cries out against the way people have treated him because he is Jewish.

SHYLOCK: *Hath not a Jew eyes? Hath not a Jews hands, organs, dimensions, senses, affections, passions? Fed with the same food, hurt with the same weapons, subject to the same diseases, healed by the same means, warmed and cooled by the same winter and summer as a Christian is? If you prick us, do we not bleed? If you tickle us, do we not laugh? If you poison us, do we not die? And if you wrong us, shall we not revenge?*

(III.i.48–55)

What point is Shylock making with this series of questions? Put his speech in your own words, using modern English.

The Merchant of Venice

In Act III, scene v, Launcelot tells Jessica that she's going to hell because she's not Christian. Her only hope, he says, is that her mother cheated on her father, which would mean that she's not really her father's daughter (and thus she doesn't share his religion).

What are your thoughts on the matter? Do you think people's religious beliefs determine what happens to them after they die? Write a paragraph about your opinion.

The Merchant of Venice

Neither Bassanio nor Antonio can repay Shylock in time, so Shylock goes to court to demand a pound of Antonio's flesh. Portia disguises herself as a lawyer and judges the case. She urges Shylock to show mercy, and Bassanio offers to pay twice the amount owed on the spot, or ten times the amount sometime in the future. But Shylock can't be convinced to change his mind. Portia admits that according to the contract, Antonio must give up a pound of his flesh. But, at the last minute, she finds a loophole. **What do you think this loophole is? In what fair way can Antonio be saved?**

The Merchant of Venice

In a comic interlude, a father and son ask a favor of Bassanio, interrupting each other constantly:

GOBBO: *Here's my son, sir, a poor boy—*
LAUNCELOT: *Not a poor boy, sir, but the rich Jew's man that would, sir, as my father shall specify—*
GOBBO: *He hath a great infection, sir, as one would say, to serve—*
LAUNCELOT: *Indeed the short and the long is, I serve the Jew and have a desire, as my father shall specify—*
GOBBO: *His master and he, saving your worship's reverence, are scarce cater-cousins—*

(II.ii.111–118)

Using these lines as a model, write your own comic dialogue in which two characters constantly interrupt each other.

The Merchant of Venice

In Act V, Lorenzo draws a clear distinction between people who love music and people who aren't moved by it. He says that the latter can't be trusted:

LORENZO: *The man that hath no music in himself,*
Nor is not moved with concord of sweet sounds,
Is fit for treason, stratagems, and spoils.
The motions of his spirit are dull as night,
And his affections dark as Erebus.
Let no such man be trusted.
(V.i.81–86)

What do you think about people who don't love music? Are you one of them? Write a paragraph on the subject.

Shakespeare Coined the Phrase . . .

"salad days":

CLEOPATRA: *My salad days,*
When I was green in judgment, cold in blood,
To say as I said then!
(I.v.73–75)

As the Shakespeare expert Michael Macrone points out, "salad days" is often used to mean "youth," but in the play *Antony and Cleopatra,* Cleopatra simply uses *salad* as a metaphor to say that when she loved Caesar, she was naïve ("green in judgment") and as "cold" as lettuce.

Think back on an embarrassing episode in your own life, and describe it with a food metaphor. Use Cleopatra's words as a frame:

My ______ days, when I was ______, ______, to say as I said then!

Shakespeare Coined the Phrase . . .

"spotless reputation":

MOWBRAY: *My dear dear lord,*
The purest treasure mortal times afford
Is spotless reputation—that away,
Men are but gilded loam or painted clay.
A jewel in a ten-times barr'd-up chest
Is a bold spirit in a loyal breast.
Mine honour is my life; both grow in one:
Take honour from me, and my life is done:
Then, dear my liege, mine honour let me try;
In that I live and for that will I die.
(I.i.176–185)

Put Mowbray's speech from *Richard II* in your own words, using modern English.

Julius Caesar

In the second scene of *Julius Caesar,* Cassius, a general, is angry and jealous after Caesar is crowned king. In the following speech, he tries to convince his friend Brutus that Caesar is no better than Brutus. **Put this speech in your own words, using modern English.**

CASSIUS: *Men at some times are masters of their fates.*
The fault, dear Brutus, is not in our stars
But in ourselves, that we are underlings.
(I.ii.140–142)

Julius Caesar

Strange events foreshadow Julius Caesar's death. **Explain these strange events in your own words, using modern English.**

CASCA: *Against the Capitol I met a lion,*
Who glared upon me and went surly by,
Without annoying me. And there were drawn
Upon a heap a hundred ghostly women,
Transformed with their fear, who swore they saw
Men all in fire walk up and down the streets.
And yesterday the bird of night did sit
Even at noon-day upon the marketplace,
Hooting and shrieking.
(I.iii.20–28)

Julius Caesar

In the second act of *Julius Caesar*, Brutus has almost decided to kill Caesar. He says that from the moment you decide to do something horrible until the moment you actually do it, everything feels like a bad dream:

BRUTUS: *Between the acting of a dreadful thing*
And the first motion, all the interim is
Like a phatasma or a hideous dream.
(II.i.63–65)

Have you ever had this feeling? Have you ever decided to do something bad and then waited nervously and guiltily until the moment came to do it? Write a paragraph about what you decided to do and how you felt at the time.

Shakespeare Coined the Phrase . . .

"a dish fit for the gods":

BRUTUS: . . . *And, gentle friends*
Let's kill him boldly but not wrathfully.
Let's carve him as a dish fit for the gods,
Not hew him as a carcass fit for hounds.
(II.i.173–176)

Contrast the use of this phrase in *Julius Caesar* to our modern use of it. How do the usages differ?

Julius Caesar

Portia, Brutus's wife, senses that something is bothering her husband. But every time she asks him what's wrong, he brushes her off or tells her he's just tired (in reality, he's worried because he's decided to kill Caesar).

Write a paragraph about a time when you've been in a similar situation—a time when you sensed that someone you loved was keeping a secret from you, or a time when you kept a secret from someone you loved.

Julius Caesar

Furious at her husband for refusing to tell her the truth, Portia asks Brutus whether he considers her his wife or his "harlot." **Put her speech in your own words, using modern English.**

PORTIA: . . . *Am I yourself*
But, as it were, in sort or limitation,
To keep with you at meals, comfort your bed,
And talk to you sometimes? Dwell I but in the suburbs
Of your good pleasure? If it be no more,
Portia is Brutus' harlot, not his wife.
(II.I.284–289)

Julius Caesar

When a loyal friend of Caesar's named Mark Antony learns that Brutus and the others have killed Caesar, he pretends to shift his loyalty to Brutus while Brutus is in the room. But when Antony is left alone with Caesar's corpse, he expresses his grief and fury and predicts dire consequences for Italy. He says mothers will get used to seeing their babies cut to pieces by war, and Caesar's ghost will wreak havoc:

ANTONY: Blood and destruction shall be so in use,
And dreadful objects so familiar,
That mothers shall but smile when they behold
Their infants quartered with the hands of war. . .
And Caesar's spirit, ranging for revenge,
With Ate by his side come hot from hell,
Shall in these confines with a monarch's voice
Cry "Havoc!" and let slip the dogs of war . . .
(III.i.273—280)

Imagine that one of your best friends has been killed. Write a speech that captures how you would respond. Fill it with anger and sadness, as Brutus does.

Julius Caesar

When a crowd demands to know why Caesar has been killed, Brutus responds:

BRUTUS: *If then that friend demand why Brutus rose against Caesar, this is my answer: not that I loved Caesar less, but that I loved Rome more.*
(III.ii.20–21)

What do you think Brutus means by this? Do you think this explanation, if true, is a reasonable one?

Julius Caesar

After Brutus speaks to the crowd, Antony makes a speech. An excerpt:

ANTONY: *[Caesar] was my friend, faithful and just to me.*
But Brutus says he was ambitious,
And Brutus is an honorable man.
He hath brought many captives home to Rome
Whose ransoms did the general coffers fill.
Did this in Caesar seem ambitious?
When that the poor have cried, Caesar hath wept.
Ambition should be made of sterner stuff.
Yet Brutus says he was ambitious,
And Brutus is an honorable man.
(III.ii.83–92)

If you had to choose one word that encapsulates the tone of this speech, which word would you choose? Write a paragraph about why you chose the word you did, citing specific words and phrases from the excerpt.

Julius Caesar

In this sinister dialogue, a group of men decide who has to be killed—including several of their siblings.

ANTONY: *These many, then, shall die. Their names are pricked.*
OCTAVIUS (to LEPIDUS): *Your brother too must die. Consent you, Lepidus?*
LEPIUDUS: *I do consent—*
OCTAVIUS: *Prick him down, Antony.*
LEPIDUS: *Upon condition Publius shall not live,*
Who is your sister's son, Mark Antony.
ANTONY: *He shall not live. Look, out with a spot I damn him.*
(IV.i.1–7)

Using this dialogue as inspiration, write a scene of your own in which a group of men hatch an ominous plan. Set the scene anywhere you want (a casino? a junkyard? a restaurant?) and in any time period you want.

Julius Caesar

When Brutus is alone one night, the ghost of Caesar visits him. **Put Brutus's response in your own words, using modern English.**

BRUTUS: . . . *Art thou any thing?*
Art thou some god, some angel, or some devil
That makest my blood cold and my hair to star?
Speak to me what thou art.
(IV.iii.281–284)

Julius Caesar

When Antony confronts Brutus and Cassius on the battlefield, he hurls simile after simile at them:

ANTONY: *Villains, you did not so when your vile daggers*
Hacked on another in the sides of Caesar.
You showed your teeth like apes, and fawned like hounds,
And bowed like bondsmen, kissing Caesar's feet,
Whilst damnéd Casca, like a cur, behind
Struck Caesar on the neck. O you flatterers!
(V.i.40–45)

Why does Antony compare his enemies to "apes," dogs, and servants? What do his similes suggest about Brutus and Cassius? Write a paragraph of analysis.

Julius Caesar

Because he thinks his side has lost the battle, Cassius despairs and orders his servant to kill him. A few lines later, though, we find out that the battle wasn't lost after all. Imagine you are one of Cassius's friends, and write a paragraph in the first person in which you express your sadness over Cassius's unnecessary death.

Julius Caesar

When Brutus realizes that the battle really has been lost, he decides that suicide is the only noble response:

BRUTUS: *It is more worthy to leap in ourselves*
Than tarry till they push us. Good Volumnius,
Thou know'st that we two went to school together.
Even for that our love of old, I prithee,
Hold thou my sword hilts, whilst I run on it.
VOLUMNIUS: *That's not an office for a friend, my lord.*
(V.v.24–29)

Volumnius refuses, but a man named Strato accedes to Brutus's request and holds the sword while Brutus impales himself on it, killing himself.

If you were Volumnius or Strato, how would you have behaved? Would you have helped or refused the desperate Brutus? Write a paragraph explaining what you would have done and why.

Shakespeare Coined the Phrase . . .

"strange bedfellows":

TRINICULO: . . . *Legged like a man, and his fins like arms! Warm, o' my troth! I do now let loose my opinion; hold it no longer: this is no fish, but an islander, that hath lately suffered by a thunderbolt.*

(thunder)

Alas, the storm is come again! My best way is to creep under his gaberdine; there is no other shelter hereabouts: misery acquaints a man with strange bedfellows. I will here shroud till the dregs of the storm be past.

(II.ii.33–41)

Triniculo speaks these words in *The Tempest* after coming across Caliban; he does not know whether Caliban is human or fish. Because of the storm, Triniculo lies down next to Caliban—he literally has a strange bedfellow. Today we use the phrase to refer to any odd pairing.

Come up with four "strange bedfellow" pairings of your own.

Shakespeare Coined the Phrase . . .

"too much of a good thing":

ORLANDO: *Then love me, Rosalind.*
ROSALIND: *Yes, faith, will I, Fridays and Saturdays and all.*
ORLANDO: *And wilt thou have me?*
ROSALIND: *Ay, and twenty such.*
ORLANDO: *What sayest thou?*
ROSALIND: *Are you not good?*
ORLANDO: *I hope so.*
ROSALIND: *Why then, can one desire too much of a good thing?*
(IV.i. 98–105)

In this scene from *As You Like It,* Rosalind suggests that if it's good to have one lover, it's better to have twenty. After all, it's hard to have too much of a good thing. What are your thoughts on the matter? Are twenty boyfriends or girlfriends better than one? Why or why not?

King Lear

At the beginning of *King Lear,* Lear asks his three daughters to tell him how much they love him. He will divide his kingdom among them according to how they respond. His daughters Goneril and Regan launch into melodramatic speeches. Goneril says she holds him "dearer than eyesight, space, and liberty," and Regan says she finds happiness only in her father's love. But Cordelia, Lear's youngest daughter, says, "I love your majesty / According to my bond, no more nor less." In other words, she loves him as a daughter should love her father, no more or less.

Suppose you were asked to defend Cordelia's reply and argue that it proves she loves her father more than Goneril and Regan love him. How would you defend her?

King Lear

After Cordelia refuses to flatter her father, he disowns her and says she won't receive her inheritance. Even though Cordelia is fatherless and penniless, the King of France still asks for her hand in marriage. As Cordelia leaves her father's court, she makes a speech to her sisters. **Put her speech in your own words, using modern English.**

CORDELIA: *I know you what you are,*
And like a sister am most loath to call
Your faults as they are named. Love well our father.
(I.i.271–273)

King Lear

As soon as they are alone, Goneril and Regan bash their father. **Put Goneril's scornful speech in your own words, using modern English.**

GONERIL: *The best and soundest of his time hath been but rash. Then must we look from his age to receive not alone the imperfections of long-engrafted condition, but therewithal the unruly waywardness that infirm and choleric years bring with them.*
(I.i.295–299)

King Lear

In Shakespeare's day, illegitimate children—that is, children born outside of a marriage—were often scorned. Edmund, the illegitimate son of Gloucester in *King Lear*, wonders why society looks down on "bastards" (illegitimate children) like himself, when they are just as smart and well formed as legitimate children:

EDMUND: *Why "bastard"? Wherefore "base"?*
When my dimensions are as well compact,
My mind as generous, and my shape as true
As honest madam's issue?
(I.ii.6–9)

What is our society's attitude toward illegitimate children? Do you think it is totally different from the attitude of Shakespeare's society? How has the meaning of the word *bastard* changed over time? Write a paragraph answering these questions.

King Lear

When Gloucester suggests that the alignment of the stars is to blame for recent unhappy events, Edmund scoffs at the way humans blame their flaws on fate or the stars:

EDMUND: . . . *When we are*
sick in fortune—often the surfeit of our own behavior—we
make guilty of our disasters the sun, the moon, and the
stars, as if we were villains by necessity, fools by heavenly
compulsion, knaves, thieves, and treachers by spherical
predominance, drunkards, liars, and adulterers by an
enforced obedience of planetary influence, and all that we
are evil in by a divine thursting-on.
(I.ii.112–119)

Do you think some of our flaws and personality traits are beyond our control? Do you believe in fate or astrology? Or, like Edmund, do you think that believing in fate is just a convenient way to deny responsibility for your actions? Write a paragraph about our beliefs.

King Lear

Fools were court jesters who could say whatever they wanted, as long as what they said was funny. King Lear's fool makes the following speech to the king. Put it in your own words, using modern English.

FOOL: *Mark it, nuncle.*
Have more than thou showest,
Speak less than thou knowest,
Lend less than thou owest,
Ride more than thou goest,
Learn more than thou trowest,
Set less than thou throwest,
Leave thy drink and thy whore
And keep in-a-door,
And thou shalt have more
Than two tens to a score.
(I.iv.103–113)

King Lear

When Goneril treats her father with disrespect, he hurls curses at her, saying he hopes she'll be unable to have children. If she does have children, he says, he hopes they'll be wicked torments who make her cry.

LEAR: *Dry up in her the organs of increase,*
And from her derogate body never spring
A babe to honor her. If she must teem,
Create her child of spleen, that it may live
And be a thwart disnatured torment to her.
Let it stamp wrinkles in her brow of youth,
With cadent tears fret channels in her cheeks,
Turn all her mother's pains and benefits
To laughter and contempt, that she may feel— . . .
How sharper than a serpent's tooth it is
To have a thankless child.
(I.iv.265–276)

Imagine getting into a terrible fight with one of your parents. Write ten lines of angry dialogue in the voice of this parent.

King Lear

Kent, furious with Oswald, comes up with a unique insult:

KENT: *Thou whoreson zed, thou unnecessary letter!*
(II.ii.57)

What does this insult mean? Try to explain it, using modern English.

King Lear

Goneril and Regan treat their father like a child, condescending to him, ordering him to be quiet, and trying to strip him of the small dignities he clings to. In his sadness and bewilderment, Lear tries and fails to think of how he can avenge himself on his daughters:

LEAR: *I will have such revenges on you both*
That all the world shall—I will do such things—
What they are yet I know not, but they shall be
The terrors of the earth. You think I'll weep?
No, I'll not weep.

(II.iv.270–274)

Imagine you've been mistreated by your (future) children. Write a speech in which you respond to them as Lear does to his children.

King Lear

Maddened by his daughters' cruelty, King Lear goes outside in a terrible storm. Kent urges him to take shelter, but Lear says the torment of the storm is distracting him from the pain his daughters are causing him.

Think about a situation in which you felt distressed. How did you distract yourself from your feelings? Write a paragraph about it.

Shakespeare Coined the Phrase . . .

"more sinned against than sinning:"

Out in the storm, King Lear protests, "I am a man / More sinned against than sinning" (III.ii.57–58).

Write about a person, either a public figure or someone in your own life, whom you think treats others better than she or he is treated in return.

King Lear

Because he covets his father's land, Edmund tells Regan and her husband, Cornwall, that Gloucester is aiding King Lear. He knows this will enrage them and they will rob Gloucester of his possessions. In fact, Cornwall and Regan are so furious that they gouge out Gloucester's eyes. The audience must watch the atrocity being performed onstage. It is one of the most disturbingly violent scenes in theater.

Write about a moment of violence in a movie or a play that disturbed you or struck you as gratuitous.

King Lear

The real villains of *King Lear* are Goneril and Regan. They are violent, cruel, ambitious, adulterous, and disloyal. They are portrayed as far more evil than any men in the play. Goneril's husband, Albany, eventually grows horrified at his wife's behavior, asking her, "What have you done? / Tigers, not daughters, what have you performed?" (IV.ii.38–39). Audiences in Shakespeare's day would have found the behavior of Goneril and Regan particularly shocking, since they were not used to seeing women portrayed as violent aggressors. Even Cordelia, the heroine, is strong. Despite her gentleness, she is said to be a "better soldier" than her husband, the king of France.

Do you think women are portrayed very differently today than they were in Shakespeare's day? Are characters like Goneril and Regan still the exception? Or are women often portrayed as strong, ambitious, and sometimes even cruel and violent? Explain your opinion, citing examples that back it up.

King Lear

If you were casting a movie version of *King Lear*, which actresses would you pick to play Goneril and Regan? Why?

King Lear

Shakespeare is always relevant to the era in which he's read. For instance, take these words of Goneril's: "Fools do those villains pity who are punished / Ere they have done their mischief" (IV.ii.53–54). In other words, only fools pity villains who are punished before they have committed their crimes.

Comment on how you think these words are relevant to the current political situation in the United States.

Shakespeare Coined the Phrase . . .

"full circle":

EDMUND: *The wheel is come full circle. I am here.*
(V.iii.180)

Contrast the use of this phrase in *King Lear* to our modern use of it. How do the usages differ?

King Lear

Goneril writes a letter to Edmund, which Edgar reads to Gloucester. Put the letter in your own words, using modern English.

Let our reciprocal vows be remembered. You have many opportunities to cut him off. If your will want not, time and place will be fruitfully offered. There is nothing to be done if he return the conqueror. Then am I the prisoner and his bed my gaol, from the loathed warmth whereof deliver me, and supply the place for your labor. Your—wife, so I would say—affectionate servant, and for you her own for venture,

Goneril.

(IV.vi.249–257)

Shakespeare Coined the Phrase . . .

"a tower of strength":

KING RICHARD: . . . *the King's name is a tower of strength,*
Which they upon the adverse faction want.
(V.iii.13–14)

Write about someone in your life whom you consider a tower of strength.

Shakespeare Coined the Phrase . . .

"what the dickens":

MRS. PAGE: *I cannot tell you what the dickens his name is my husband had him of. What do you call your knight's name, sirrah?*
(III.ii.19–20)

Think of at least three other expressions that mean the same thing as "what the dickens" and sound similarly quaint to the modern ear.

Much Ado About Nothing

In the following exchange, Leonato jokes about his daughter, Hero, when Don Pedro asks about her:

DON PEDRO: *I think this is your daughter.*
LEONATO: *Her mother hath many times told me so.*
BENEDICK: *Were you in doubt, sir, that you asked her?*
LEONATO: *Signor Benedick, no, for then were you a child.*
(I.i.84–87)

Put Leonato's two jokes in your own words, using modern English.

Much Ado About Nothing

Don John, Don Pedro's villainous brother, is a gloomy person by nature. He says, "though I / cannot be said to be a flattering honest man, it must not be / denied but I am a plain-dealing villain" (I.iii.23–25). In other words, he thinks he deserves some credit for being honest about his true nature.

Do you agree with Don John that it's best not to put on a show of happiness if you're in a terrible mood or pretend to be kind if you're really a mean person? Is honesty always the best policy in terms of how you present yourself? Or do you think that it's better to seem happy and kind even when you're not? Explain.

Much Ado About Nothing

After Claudio falls in love with Hero, Benedick bemoans the change in his lovesick friend:

BENEDICK: . . . *He was wont to speak plain and to the purpose, like an honest man and a soldier, and now he is turned orthography; his words are a very fantastical banquet, just so many strange dishes.*

(II.iii.16–19)

How does Benedick characterize Claudio's manner of speech before he fell in love? How does Claudio speak now, according to Benedick, after having fallen in love? Explain.

Much Ado About Nothing

Benedick lists the qualities a woman must have in order for him to be interested in her:

BENEDICK: . . . *Rich shall she be, that's*
certain; wise, or I'll none; virtuous, or I'll never cheapen
her; fair, or I'll never look on her; mild, or come not near
me; noble, or not I for an angel; of good discourse, an
excellent musician, and her hair shall be of what color it
please God.

(II.iii.26–31)

What are your own requirements in an ideal mate? List them, attempting to use language similar to Benedick's.

Much Ado About Nothing

Claudio, Leonato, and Don Pedro conspire to trick Beatrice and Benedick into falling in love with each other. They make sure Benedick can overhear them, then talk loudly about how desperately Beatrice loves Benedick. **Put their conversation in your own words, using modern English.**

CLAUDIO: *Down upon her knees she falls, weeps, sobs, beats her heart, tears her hair, prays, curses: "O sweet Benedick! God give me patience!"*
LEONATO: *She doth indeed, my daughter says so, and the ecstasy hath so much overborne her that my daughter is sometime afeared she will do a desperate outrage to herself. It is very true.*
(II.iii.133–139)

Much Ado About Nothing

Hero and her servants, Ursula and Margaret, are in on the conspiracy to make Beatrice and Benedick fall in love. They talk in the orchard, making sure Beatrice can overhear them. Put their conversation in your own words, using modern English.

URSULA: *But are you sure*
That Benedick loves Beatrice so entirely?
HERO: *So says the Prince and my new-trothéd lord.*
URSULA: *And did they bid you tell her of it, madam?*
HERO: *They did entreat me to acquaint her of it,*
But I persuaded them, if they loved Benedick,
To wish him wrestle with affection
And never to let Beatrice know of it.

(III.i.37–43)

Much Ado About Nothing

Much Ado About Nothing is full of jokes about sex. What is Margaret joking about here?

HERO: *God give me joy to wear it, for my heart is exceeding heavy.*
MARGARET: *'Twill be heavier soon by the weight of a man.*
HERO: *Fie upon thee! Art not ashamed?*
(III.iv.21–23)

Much Ado About Nothing

Don John and his associates trick Claudio and Don Pedro into thinking that Hero is not a virgin—that she has, in fact, slept with a commoner thousands of times. Instead of breaking off his engagement with Hero, Claudio waits until the wedding ceremony is in progress and then calls Hero a slut in front of her friends and family.

Can you imagine a situation in which you'd be as enraged as Claudio? What would your fiancé have to do in order to make you dump him or her at the altar?

Much Ado About Nothing

After Claudio leaves Hero at the altar, the friar advises Hero's family to pretend that she's died of a broken heart. This way, he says, Claudio will come to regret what he did. The friar says we only appreciate what we have after we've lost it:

FRIAR FRANCIS: *What we have we prize not to the worth*
Whiles we enjoy it, but being lacked and lost,
Why then we rack the value, then we find
The virtue that possession would not show us
Whiles it was ours.

(IV.i.217–221)

Write a paragraph about something you appreciated only after you lost it.

Much Ado About Nothing

Dogberry, the chief policeman of Messina, provides comic relief. He tries to imitate the speech of noblemen, but he often gets words mixed up. In Act IV, Conrade calls him an ass, and he reacts indignantly. How does he define himself in the following speech? Put his ideas in your own words, using modern English.

DOGBERRY: . . . *masters, remember that I am an ass, though it be not*
written down, yet forget not that I am an ass.—No, thou
villain . . . I am a wise fellow and, which is more, an
officer and, which is more, a householder and, which is
more, as pretty a piece of flesh as any is in Messina, and one
that knows the law, go to,
and a rich fellow enough, go to,
and a fellow that hath had losses, and one that hath two gowns
and everything handsome about him.
(IV.ii.68–76)

Much Ado About Nothing

Leonato, speaking about his distress over what's happened to Hero, says, "there was never yet philosopher / That could endure the toothache patiently" (V.i.35–36).

What do you think Leonato means by this?

Much Ado About Nothing

Explain what is comical about the following speech spoken by Dogberry:

DOGBERRY: *Marry, sir, they have committed false report; moreover, they have spoken untruths, secondarily, they are slanders; sixth and lastly, they have belied a lady; thirdly, they have verified unjust things; and, to conclude, they are lying knaves.*

(V.i.202–206)

Much Ado About Nothing

Beatrice and Benedick engage in barbed banter even after they've admitted that they love each other. As Benedick says, they are "too wise to woo peaceably" (V.ii.58). A sample:

BENEDICK: *Sweet Beatrice, wouldst thou come when I called thee?*
BEATRICE: *Yea, Signior, and depart when you bid me.*
BENEDICK: *Oh, stay but till then!*
BEATRICE: *"Then" is spoken. Fare you well now. And yet, ere I go, let me go with that I came, which is, with knowing what hath passed between you and Claudio.*
BENEDICK: *Only foul words, and thereupon I will kiss thee.*
BEATRICE: *Foul words is but foul wind, and foul wind is but foul breath, and foul breath is noisome. Therefore I will depart unkissed.*

(V.ii.33–42)

Using this exchange as inspiration, write a dialogue between two people who love each other—and love to tease each other.

Much Ado About Nothing

If you were casting a movie version of *Much Ado About Nothing*, which actors would you pick to play Beatrice and Benedick? What is it about these actors that makes them able to portray the smart, quarrelsome, brilliant pair?

Shakespeare Coined the Phrase . . .

"the world's my oyster":

FALSTAFF: *I will not lend thee a penny.*
PISTOL: *Why then the world's mine oyster*
Which I with sword will open.
(II.ii.2–4)

In this exchange from *The Merry Wives of Windsor,* Falstaff refuses to lend Pistol any money. As a result, what does Pistol threaten to do?

Shakespeare Coined the Phrase . . .

"breathed his last":

SOMERSET: *Ah, Warwick, Montague hath breath'd his last,*
And to the latest gasp cried out for Warwick,
And said, "Commend me to my valiant brother."
(V.ii.40–42)

"Breathed his last" is one of hundreds of euphemisms for dying. (A **euphemism** is an agreeable expression that describes a disagreeable situation.) In the next five minutes, think of as many euphemisms for dying as you can.

Shakespeare Coined the Phrase . . .

"my heart on my sleeve":

IAGO: *But I will wear my heart upon my sleeve*
For daws to peck at. I am not what I am.
(I.i.66–67)

Iago suggests that baring your emotions—wearing your heart on your sleeve—is a dangerous move. If you expose your heart, you weaken yourself, thus leaving yourself open to attack. Metaphorically, birds will pick at an exposed heart just as they would at a literal heart.

In your opinion, is it better to show or to hide your true feelings? Explain.

Othello

In the first scene of *Othello,* the villainous Iago goes to the house of Brabantio, a senator and the father of Desdemona. Iago shouts up to Brabantio that Desdemona is having sex with Othello:

IAGO: *Your heart is burst, you have lost half your soul.*
Even now, now, very now, an old black ram
Is tupping your white ewe.
(I.i.89–91)

Iago loathes Othello, a celebrated general, and he wants to get Brabantio angry. In what way does he try to do this? Cite specific words and phrases in your answer.

Othello

Brabantio is shocked at the idea that his daughter, who has rejected all the young suitors in Venice, could fall in love with a black man. He insists that Desdemona would be afraid to look at Othello, much less fall in love with him, and claims that Othello must have drawn her in with some magic potion.

Have you ever dated someone your parents didn't approve of? Did they respond irrationally? Write about your experience (or, if you prefer, the experience of a friend).

Othello

When Brabantio accuses Othello of using magic to ensnare Desdemona, Othello replies by explaining how Brabantio used to invite him over and ask him to talk about his life. **According to Othello, why did Desdemona fall in love with him?**

OTHELLO: *I spoke of most disastrous chances,*
Of moving accidents by flood and field,
Of hair-breadth 'scapes i' th' imminent deadly breach,
Of being taken by the insolent foe
And sold to slavery, of my redemption thence
And portance in my traveler's history. . . .
[Desdemona] loved me for the dangers I'd passed
And I loved her that she did pity them.
This only is the witchcraft I have used.
(I.iii.135–140, 168–170)

Othello

Roderigo complains to Iago that he is sick with love for Desdemona, but Iago scoffs at him, saying that we control our own emotions and desires:

IAGO: *'Tis in ourselves that we are thus or thus.*
Our bodies are our gardens, to the which our will are
gardeners. So that if we will plant nettles or sow lettuce,
set hyssop and weed up thyme, supply it with one gender
of herbs or distract it with many—either to have it sterile
with idleness, or manured with industry—why, the power
and corrigible authority of this lies in our wills.
(I.iii.319–325)

Do you agree with Iago that we can control our feelings, or do you think falling in love is something we can control? Use examples from your own life to back up your argument.

Othello

Iago loathes Othello with every particle of his being, even though he admits that Othello is "of a constant, loving, noble nature" (II.i.83). Critics have never agreed about why Iago hates Othello so much. Samuel Taylor Coleridge famously said that "motiveless malignity" drives Iago—that is, Iago detests Othello for no reason in particular.

Have you ever disliked someone for no real reason? Why or why not? Explain.

Othello

What follows is a famous speech made by Iago. Put it in your own words, using modern English.

IAGO: *Who steals my purse steals trash. 'Tis something, nothing:*
'Twas mine, 'tis his, and has been slave to thousands.
But he that filches from me my good name
Robs me of that which enriches him
And makes me poor indeed.
(III.iii.162–166)

Othello

As part of his plan to ruin Othello's life, the cunning Iago plants seeds of doubt in Othello's mind by urging him not to be suspicious of Desdemona. Othello understands that Iago is implying something and asks him to speak honestly, but Iago pretends to be reluctant. Then he reminds Othello that Desdemona is capable of lying—after all, she lied to her father in order to marry Othello. He also suggests that one day Desdemona will long for someone of her own race. Iago advises Othello to keep his eye on Cassio, a handsome young lieutenant. Having succeeded in making Othello worry, Iago urges him not to worry.

Following this outline exactly, write a modern update of a scene in which one person plants seeds of doubt in another person's mind.

Othello

Iago claims that he recently had to share a bed with Cassio and that Cassio talked in his sleep:

IAGO: *In his sleep I heard him say "Sweet Desdemona,*
Let us be wary, let us hide our loves."
And then, sir, would he gripe and wring my hand,
Cry "O sweet creature!" and then kiss me hard,
. . . lay his leg
Over my thigh, and sigh, and kiss. . . .
OTHELLO: *Oh, monstrous! Monstrous!*
IAGO: *Nay, this was but his dream.*
OTHELLO: *But this denoted a foregone conclusion.*
(III.iii.426–429, 431–432, 434–436)

What does Iago claim Cassio's dream proves? What does he want Othello to believe it proves? Explain.

Shakespeare Coined the Phrase . . .

"the green-eyed monster":

IAGO: *Oh, beware, my lord, of jealousy!*
It is the green-eyed monster which doth mock
The meat it feeds on.
(III.iii.169–171)

Using Shakespeare's description of jealousy as a "green-eyed monster," make up evocative three-word metaphors for the following words: *lust, sloth, gluttony,* and *anger.*

Othello

Othello, now wrongly convinced that Desdemona is cheating on him with Cassio, says he wouldn't mind if the entire army had slept with her, as long as he hadn't found out about it.

Do you agree with Othello? Would you rather not know that your boyfriend or girlfriend was cheating on you and be happy in your ignorance, or would you rather find out about it and be miserable because of your knowledge? Explain.

Othello

Enraged, Othello accuses Desdemona of cheating on him, calling her a whore and saying he wishes that she'd never been born. Desdemona, shocked, tries to defend herself. Afterward, she talks to Iago and his wife, Emilia:

DESDEMONA: *Am I that name, Iago?*
IAGO: *What name, fair lady?*
DESDEMONA: *Such as she says my lord did say I was.*
EMILIA: *He called her "whore."*
(IV.ii.124–127)

What does Desdemona's reluctance to say *whore* suggest?

Othello

Casting *Othello* has always stirred up controversy. For years, white men played the role of the title character, whom Shakespeare identifies as black. Not until 1942 did American audiences see a black man play Othello. If you were casting a movie version of *Othello*, which actors would you pick to play Othello and Desdemona? Why?

Twelfth Night

Viola, a young aristocrat, is shipwrecked. Convinced that her twin brother, Sebastian, was killed in the shipwreck, Viola decides she must support herself. She disguises herself as a man named Cesario and goes to work for Orsino, a nobleman who is sick with love for Olivia, a beautiful noblewoman. Viola falls in love with Orsino but cannot confess her love for him, because she is disguised as a man. When Orsino sends Viola to woo Olivia on his behalf, Olivia falls in love with Viola, whom she thinks is a man.

Do you think convoluted plots like this one are common in the films and plays of today, or do you think most writers and directors favor realistic plots? Give examples to back up your argument.

Twelfth Night

If you were casting a movie version of *Twelfth Night*, which actors would you pick to play the twins, Viola and Sebastian? Why? What makes the actors you would choose good for the roles?

Twelfth Night

Olivia is in mourning for her brother, who recently died. Her fool (a jester) teases her about moping around:

FOOL: *Good madonna, why mournest thou?*
OLIVIA: *Good fool, for my brother's death.*
FOOL: *I think his soul is in heaven, madonna.*
OLIVIA: *I know his soul is in heaven, fool.*
FOOL: *The more fool, madonna, to mourn for your brother's soul being in heaven.*

(I.v.60–65)

Why, according to the fool, is Olivia foolish to mourn for her brother? Explain.

Twelfth Night

Malvolio, Olivia's head servant, is an uptight man who looks down on people who drink, sing, and generally enjoy themselves. Maria, another of Olivia's servants, characterizes Malvolio as a pretentious puritan who tries to act like a nobleman.

Do you know anyone who looks down on people who enjoy themselves? Do you know anyone who is snobby and affected? Write a paragraph describing one of these people.

Twelfth Night

Maria and her friends Sir Toby Belch and Sir Andrew Auguecheek conspire to trick Malvolio in a cruel way. Maria writes a letter in Olivia's handwriting, a letter in which Olivia supposedly confesses her love for Malvolio. Then Maria plants the letter where Malvolio will find it. An excerpt from the letter:

Thou canst not choose but know who I am. If thou entertainest my love, let it appear in thy smiling. Thy smiles become thee well. Therefore in my presence still smile, dear my sweet, I prithee.
(II.v.155–158)

How would you convince one of your enemies that someone was in love with him or her? Draft your own fake love letter to this enemy, real or imaginary.

Twelfth Night

Sir Andrew imagines he has a chance with Olivia. When he sees her flirting with Viola/Cesario, he is outraged. But Fabian, a servant of Olivia's, has a theory that may comfort Sir Andrew. **Put his theory in your own words, using modern English.**

FABIAN: *She did show favor to the youth in your sight only to exasperate you, to awake your dormouse valor, to put fire in your heart and brimstone in your liver.*

(III.ii.17–19)

Twelfth Night

A man named Antonio sees Viola dressed as a man and mistakes her for his good friend, Sebastian (Viola's twin brother). Viola swears that she has never met Antonio before. Crushed, Antonio makes this speech:

ANTONIO: *But oh, how vile an idol proves this god!*
Thou hast, Sebastian, done good feature shame.
In nature there's no blemish but the mind.
None can be called deformed but the unkind.
Virtue is beauty, but the beauteous evil
Are empty trunks o'erflourished by the devil.
(III.iv.332–337)

In essence, Antonio says that the only real flaws in nature are in a person's mind and soul: only cruel people can be called deformed. Someone who is both beautiful and evil is like an empty box decorated by the devil. Describe someone you know who is an "empty box"—a beautiful person with a nasty personality.

Twelfth Night

The servant Maria and her coconspirators pretend that Malvolio is insane and have him locked up. He cries out pitifully, saying, "never was man thus wronged. . . . They have laid me here in hideous darkness" (IV.ii.26–27). Later he tells the fool, "there was never a man so notoriously abused: I am as / well in my wits, Fool, as thou art" (IV.ii.77–78). **Using Malvolio's melancholy words as inspiration, write a speech of your own to be spoken by a person who has been unfairly imprisoned.**

Twelfth Night

At the end of *Twelfth Night*, Viola and Sebastian are reunited. Olivia and Sebastian agree to marry, and Orsino proposes to Viola. Despite the happiness of the impending marriages, Malvolio's rage suffuses the last moments of the play, and the tone of the last scene is ambiguous.

Describe a movie you've seen that ended on a melancholy or bittersweet note. Then explain why, in your opinion, ambiguous endings are so rare in American film.

Shakespeare Coined the Phrase . . .

"winter of our discontent":

RICHARD: *Now is the winter of our discontent*
Made glorious summer by this son of York. . . .
(I.i.1–2)

Why is it incorrect to say that *Richard III*, the play that opens with these lines, begins on a gloomy note? (Hint: read the lines very carefully.)

Shakespeare Coined the Phrase . . .

"A horse! A horse! My kingdom for a horse!":

Richard speaks this phrase in the fifth act of *Richard III.* In desperation at losing his horse in the middle of battle, he says he would give up everything if he could have a horse at this moment.

Have you ever longed for something that you normally wouldn't think about twice—the key to your car door after you've locked the keys in the car, for example? Write about the experience.

Romeo and Juliet

In the first scene of *Romeo and Juliet*, we learn of the hatred between the Capulets and the Montagues when Sampson and Gregory, servants of the Capulets, start a fight with servants of the Montagues. To provoke the Montague men, Sampson bites his thumb at them in a gesture of disrespect:

ABRAM: *Do you bit your thumb at us, sir?*
SAMPSON: *I do bite my thumb, sir.*
ABRAM: *Do you bit your thumb at us, sir? . . .*
SAMPSON: *No, sir. I do not bite my thumb at you, sir, but I bite my thumb, sir.*
GREGORY: *Do you quarrel, sir?*
ABRAM: *Quarrel, sir? No, sir.*
(I.i.39–41, 44–47)

The way in which people starting fights in Shakespeare's time sounds strikingly similar to how people start fights in our time. **Write a modern dialogue between two people about to brawl. Use lots of repetition and provoking questions, as Shakespeare does.**

Romeo and Juliet

We learn that Romeo, a Montague, is depressed. He takes walks late at night and comes home just before sunrise. He goes to his room, "shuts up his windows, locks fair daylight out" (I.i.132), and won't tell anyone what's wrong.

How do you behave when you're depressed? Do you keep to yourself, as Romeo does? Do you prefer company? Do you try to distract yourself or take your mind off the problem? Explain.

Romeo and Juliet

At the beginning of the play, Romeo is in love with Rosaline, a beautiful girl who has sworn to remain a virgin forever.

BENVOLIO: *Then she hath sworn that she will still live chaste?*
ROMEO: *She hath, and in that sparing makes huge waste,*
For beauty, starved with her severity,
Cuts beauty off from all posterity.
(I.i.211–214)

What objection against virginity is Romeo voicing? Explain.

Romeo and Juliet

Juliet's mother, Lady Capulet, announces that a man named Paris wants to marry Juliet, who is thirteen years old. Paris will attend a party that Juliet's father is throwing that night. Lady Capulet says that when she was thirteen, she was already mother to Juliet.

Imagine that you'd gotten married at age thirteen. Write a paragraph about how your life might be different.

Romeo and Juliet

Romeo and his friends Benvolio and Mercutio plan to crash Lord Capulet's party. Before they go in, Romeo speaks:

ROMEO: . . . *My mind misgives*
Some consequence yet hanging in the stars
Shall bitterly begin his fearful date
With this night's revels, and expire the term
Of a despisèd life closed in my breast
By some vile forfeit of untimely death.
(I.iv.108–113)

What do you think Romeo fears? Name the literary device Shakespeare used to describe this fear.

Romeo and Juliet

Act II, scene ii of *Romeo and Juliet* contains a line that is often misinterpreted. The line is bolded below:

JULIET: *O Romeo, Romeo!* ***Wherefore art thou Romeo?***
Deny thy father and refuse thy name.
Or, if thou wilt not, be but sworn my love,
And I'll no longer be a Capulet.
(II.ii.33–36)

Can you figure out the common misinterpretation of the line and the actual meaning of the line? Cite specific words and phrases as evidence.

Romeo and Juliet

Romeo calls up to Juliet, who is on her balcony. They talk, and Juliet begs Romeo to profess his love for her:

JULIET: *O gentle Romeo,*
If thou dost love, pronounce it faithfully.
Or if thou think'st I am too quickly won,
I'll frown and be perverse and say thee nay,
So thou wilt woo.
(II.ii.94–98)

Juliet says that if Romeo thinks she's too quick to profess her love for him, she'll play hard to get. She'll "frown and be perverse" and put him off in order to make him "woo" her.

How do you act when you like someone? Do you play games or play hard to get in order to capture the interest of the person you like, or do you try to be honest? Write about your romance tactics.

Romeo and Juliet

After a brief meeting at the Capulets' party and a conversation later that night, Romeo and Juliet marry. Can you imagine any situation in which you'd marry someone after such a brief period? Explain.

Romeo and Juliet

Shakespeare's Juliet is thirteen years old, and Romeo probably isn't much older. Some directors have ignored this fact completely, casting middle-aged actors in the title roles. If you were casting a movie version of the play, which actors would you pick to play Romeo and Juliet? Why?

Romeo and Juliet

Mercutio tells Benvolio that he, Benvolio, is a certain type of person:

MERCUTIO: *Thou art like one of those fellows that, when he enters the confines of a tavern, claps me his sword upon the table and says, "God send me no need of thee!" and, by the operation of the second cup, draws it on the drawer when indeed there is no need.*

(III.i.5–9)

What kind of guy is Benvolio, according to Mercutio?

Romeo and Juliet

Romeo gets drawn into a fight and kills Tybalt, Juliet's cousin. The prince decrees that Romeo must be banished from Verona as punishment for the murder. Romeo hides at the house of his friend, Friar Lawrence, who tries to reason with Romeo. **Put Romeo's response in your own words, using modern English.**

ROMEO: *Thou canst not speak of that thou dost not feel.*
Wert thou as young as I, Juliet thy love,
An hour but married, Tybalt murderèd,
Doting like me, and liked me banishèd,
Then mightst thou speak, then mightst thou tear thy hair
And fall upon the ground, as I do now. . . .
(III.iii.64–69)

Romeo and Juliet

After Romeo is banished, Juliet's father, who knows nothing of his daughter's marriage, tells Juliet that she must marry Paris right away. When she protests, he says he'll throw her out of the house to starve if she disobeys him. Lady Capulet refuses to take Juliet's side. After her parents leave, Juliet asks for her nurse's opinion. The nurse, who facilitated Juliet's marriage to Romeo, suggests that Juliet should marry Paris. After all, she says, Romeo isn't around, so Juliet can't enjoy him, and Paris is a handsome man. Juliet, horrified by this advice, decides she can never confide in her nurse again.

Have you ever abruptly lost faith in an adult as Juliet loses faith in her nurse? Write about the experience.

Romeo and Juliet

Juliet takes a potion that makes her appear to be dead, and her family, falling for the ruse, buries her in a tomb. Romeo hears of her supposed death, breaks into her tomb, and kills himself by drinking poison. Juliet awakes, finds Romeo dead, and kills herself with a knife. The prince blames the tragedy on the feud between the Capulets and the Montagues. **Put his accusation in your own words, using modern English.**

PRINCE: *Capulet! Montague!*
See what a scourge is laid upon your hate
That heaven finds means to kill your joys with love!
(V.iii.291–293)

Sonnet 1

Many of Shakespeare's sonnets are addressed to a young man. In Sonnet 1, the speaker chastises the young man:

From fairest creatures we desire increase
That thereby beauty's rose might never die
But as the riper should by time decease,
His tender heir might bear his memory;
But thou, contracted to thine own bright eyes,
Feed'st thy light's flame with self-substantial fuel,
Making a famine where abundance lies. . . .

What crime has the young man committed, according to the speaker?

Sonnet 20

In Sonnet 20, the speaker says that because Mother Nature made his beloved a man, they can't sleep together. Still, the speaker will persist in loving him:

But since she [Mother Nature] pricked thee out for women's pleasure,
Mine be thy love, and thy love's use their treasure.

What distinction does the speaker draw in these lines?

Sonnet 23

An excerpt:

As an unperfect actor on the stage
Who with his fear is put besides his part . . .

So I, for fear of trust, forget to say
The perfect ceremony of love's rite . . .

Analyze these lines. What troubles the speaker? To what does he compare himself?

Sonnet 29

An excerpt:

Haply I think on thee, and then my state,
Like to the lark at break of day arising
From sullen earth, sings hymns at heaven's gate.
For thy sweet love remembered such wealth brings
That then I scorn to change my state with kings.

When he feels depressed, the speaker thinks of his beloved and remembers that he wouldn't change places even with a king. Who or what do you think about when you're depressed? How does this person or thing make you feel—better or worse? Explain.

Sonnet 65

In Sonnet 65, the speaker asks how beauty and youth can be saved from the ravages of time. What is the solution? The sonnet concludes:

O none, unless this miracle have might:
That in black ink my love may still shine bright.

What, according to this conclusion, is the one way to preserve youth and beauty forever?

Sonnet 116

An excerpt:

Love's not time's fool, though rosy lips and cheeks
Within his bending sickle's compass come;
Love alters not with his brief hours and weeks,
But bears it out even to the edge of doom.

According to the speaker of this sonnet, what effect does time have on love?

Sonnet 138

An excerpt:

When my love swears that she is made of truth
I do believe her though I know she lies,
That she might think me some untutored youth
Unlearnèd in the world's false subtleties.

The speaker of this sonnet knows his lover is cheating on him, even though she swears she's not. Why do you think he pretends to believe her? Cite specific words and phrases as evidence.

Bowdlerized Shakespeare

Shakespeare heartily embraces the naughty, violent, and offensive. Racial slurs, dirty jokes, prostitutes, drunks, and incestuous uncles (not to mention thirteen-year-old girls longing to lose their virginity) populate his works. In 1818, a woman named Harriet Bowdler anonymously published *The Family Shakespeare*, "in which nothing is added to the original text; but those words and expressions are omitted which cannot with propriety be read aloud in a family." The volume achieved great popularity in the Victorian age. As a result of Bowdler's efforts, the word *bowdlerize* has entered the English language. **Based on the information above, try defining the word.**

At the Theater

In Shakespeare's day, going to see a play was not a sober cultural event. Calling out to the actors onstage was common, as was talking to your friends during the performance and buying beer and nuts from vendors.

Describe your last experience at the movies. What did you wear and do? What was the mood of the audience? What are your impressions of moviegoing?

Titles from Shakespeare

Innumerable authors have taken titles for their novels, poems, movies, and other works from Shakespeare (*Brave New World*, *What Dreams May Come*, and *Things Fall Apart*, to name just a few). If you wrote a novel and wanted to use a phrase from Shakespeare's work as its title, which phrase would you choose, and why?

You Onstage

Consider all the characters from Shakespeare you've read about. Which one would you most like to play onstage, and why?

Answers

1. Answers will vary.
2. Translations should resemble this one:

   Thrice noble lord, please excuse me for another night or two. Or if you can't do that, excuse me at least until sundown. Your doctors, who are worried that you might have a relapse, have specifically forbidden me to sleep with you.

3. Tranio thinks that there's nothing to be gained from doing things that don't please you—that is, if you hate math and metaphysics, you shouldn't force yourself to study them. You should only spend as much time on them as you can stand.
4. Translations should resemble this one:

   Petruchio, I can help you find a wife who's rich, young, beautiful, and brought up as a gentlewoman should be. Her only flaw, and it's a big flaw, is that she is unbearable—a total witch.

5. When Hortensio told Katherine that she was using the wrong frets and tried to correct her fingering, she jumped up and said, "Frets? I'll give you frets!" She clobbered Hortensio with the lute so that his head went right through the instrument. He stood in a daze, looking through the hole as if he was caught in the stocks, while Katherine called him "worthless

fiddler," "twanging twerp," and twenty more hateful names. It was as if she'd prepared insults beforehand.

6. Petruchio behaves this way because he wants to break Katherine's spirit. By treating her badly and forcing her to do things against her will, he hopes to show her that he's the boss.

7. Katherine says that the sun isn't the sun if Petruchio says it isn't, and the moon changes according to his mind. She says everything is what he says it is, and "so it shall be" for her, too. In essence, Katherine is giving up the fight. By no longer struggling against Petruchio, trying to exert her own will, or expressing her own opinions, she is agreeing to let him be the dominant one in the relationship.

8. Answers will vary.

9. Answers will vary.

10. Answers will vary. Jaques's seven stages are "the infant," "the whining school-boy," "the lover, / Sighing like furnace," "a soldier," "the justice," a man "[w]ith spectacles on nose and pouch on side," and, finally, a being of "second childishness and mere oblivion."

11. Answers will vary.

12. Answers will vary.

13. She wants to erase all traces of womanliness from herself and become an entirely cruel, masculine being. She does not want to feel any remorse or regret for what she's about to do. She asks the demon "spirits" that assist murderous, "mortal thoughts" to turn the milk in her breasts into poison. In short, Lady Macbeth wants to suffuse herself "from the crown to the toe" with a violent, murderous spirit.

14. Answers will vary, but students may suggest that, in this context, "the be-all and the end-all" is the action that settles events permanently. Macbeth wonders if killing the king is all he has to do in order to capture the crown for himself, or if unforeseen consequences might arise. If killing Duncan would provide a tidy solution, Macbeth says, he would gladly risk the afterlife to do it.

15. Translations should resemble this one:

    I have breastfed a baby, and I know how tender it is to love the baby that's nursing. I would, while the baby was smiling up at my face, have plucked my nipple from its toothless mouth and smashed its brains out against a wall if I had sworn to do that in the same way that you have sworn to do this.

16. She uses the phrase to suggest that Macbeth is too compassionate, too full of the "milk of human kindness." He craves power, and he is ambitious, but he doesn't have the viciousness that should accompany these qualities. Today, we use the phrase to praise particularly kind people—quite the opposite of Lady Macbeth's intention.

17. Macbeth could use "sorry" to mean "sickening" or "upsetting," but he could also mean to suggest regret for what he has done. He could be employing dark humor, making light of what he knows is a desperate situation; "a sorry sight" is a pretty understated way to describe someone who's just murdered a king.

18. Translations should resemble this one:

    Drinking turns your nose red, puts you to sleep, and makes you urinate. Lust, sir, it turns on and turns off. Drinking stimulates desire but takes away your ability to perform. Therefore, too much drink is like a con artist when it comes to your sex drive. It persuades you and discourages you; it gives you an erection but doesn't let you keep it. It makes you dream about erotic experiences, but then it leaves you asleep and needing to pee.

19. Macduff suggests that, because she is a woman, Lady Macbeth is too delicate to hear the news of the king's death. He thinks the news would kill her if he told it to her. This is ironic, because it was Lady Macbeth who insisted on the murder of Duncan and pushed her husband to commit it. She is the last person who would be shocked by news of the murder, and she is certainly not a weak or "gentle lady."
20. Answers will vary.
21. Answers will vary.
22. Answers will vary.
23. Answers will vary.
24. Answers will vary.
25. Answers will vary.
26. Answers will vary.
27. Students may say that the repetition highlights Macduff's shock at the news. He doesn't want to believe that his whole family has been slaughtered. Even though Ross has explained the disaster quite clearly, Macduff can't take it in.
28. Answers will vary.
29. Answers will vary.

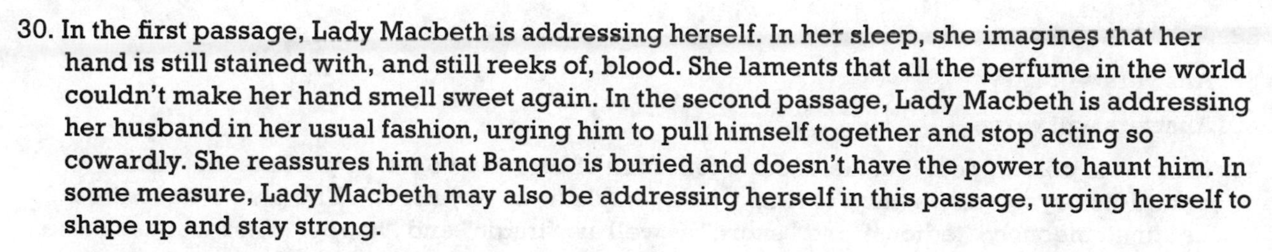

30. In the first passage, Lady Macbeth is addressing herself. In her sleep, she imagines that her hand is still stained with, and still reeks of, blood. She laments that all the perfume in the world couldn't make her hand smell sweet again. In the second passage, Lady Macbeth is addressing her husband in her usual fashion, urging him to pull himself together and stop acting so cowardly. She reassures him that Banquo is buried and doesn't have the power to haunt him. In some measure, Lady Macbeth may also be addressing herself in this passage, urging herself to shape up and stay strong.

31. Answers will vary.

32. Answers will vary.

33. Answers will vary.

34. In *Henry VIII*, the speaker literally means "for the sake of goodness." He appeals to the audience's kindness, asking them to let the play make them sad, as it's supposed to. Today, we use the phrase to indicate our annoyance, as in "Oh, for goodness' sake, stop making me read *Henry VIII*."

35. Answers will vary.

36. Answers will vary.

37. Translations should resemble this one:

> I know you snuck away from Fairyland and, disguised as a shepherd, spent all day playing straw pipes and signing love songs to your girlfriend, Phillida. Why did you come back from faraway India? For no other reason than that you wanted to see that butch Amazon Hippolyta, your boot-wearing mistress and your warrior lover. Now that she's marrying Theseus, you've come to celebrate their marriage.

38. Answers will vary.

39. Answers will vary.

40. Answers will vary.

41. Theseus is pointing out that the description is full of **oxymorons**, or phrases that join contradictory words ("jumbo shrimp," for example, is an oxymoron). The play is described as simultaneously "tedious" and "short," as well as "tragic" and "happy." Theseus says these descriptions are like "hot ice" (another oxymoron).

42. Shakespeare wants us to laugh at this speech. The rhymes are absurdly childish ("dead" and "fled," "light" and flight), Bottom repeats his assertion that he's dead over and over, the rhyme scheme is abrupt and choppy, and the last line, with its repetition of "die," is sheer comedy.

43. Answers will vary.

44. Answers will vary.

45. Translations should resemble this one:

> Why she, even she—oh God, an animal that can't think would have mourned its mate longer than she did!—married my uncle, my father's brother, who's about as much like my father as I am like Hercules.

46. Hamlet suggests that Claudius is "more than kin," meaning that Claudius is more than a cousin—he is now Hamlet's stepfather. Claudius is "less than kind" because he is rude. The word kind also meant "natural" in Shakespeare's time, and by using it Hamlet implies that Claudius's marriage to Gertrude, his former sister-in-law, is unnatural.

47. Answers will vary.

48. He means that the king was murdered by his brother, Claudius, who is now king.

49. It was King Hamlet's habit to take a nap in his orchard each afternoon. Claudius snuck up on the king and poured a vial of henbane poison into his ear. It caused a scary rash to break out all over King Hamlet, covering his body with a vile and revolting crust. In this way, Claudius stole King Hamlet's life, kingship, and wife.

50. The phrase "brevity is the soul of wit" means that conciseness is at the heart of humor. But Polunius is anything but concise: he rambles on interminably about "why day is day" and why night is night, then wastes time explaining that to ramble on is itself "nothing but to waste night, day and time." Finally, he explains in four different ways that Hamlet is insane.

51. Answers will vary.

52. Answers will vary, but students may say that Hamlet is initially angry at himself ("what an ass am I!") and then quickly grows sarcastic ("This is most brave"). His self-loathing is apparent when he compares himself to a "whore" who curses in the streets.

53. Death scares us because we don't know what's on the other side of it. We're not sure what dreams we'll encounter after we've died; in fact, we don't have any idea what death will be like at all. Something horrible may await us in death or after death.

54. Students might mention movie voice-overs, in which characters address the audience directly. Examples will vary.

55. Answers will vary.

56. In this passage from *Hamlet*, "piece of work" means "play." We usually use "piece of work" to refer to someone who is quirky or slightly crazy, as in, "He's a real piece of work."

57. Answers will vary.

58. Translations should resemble this one:

> Show me the man who is not enslaved to passion, and I'll put him close to my heart—in my heart of hearts—as I do you.

59. Answers will vary.

60. Answers will vary.

61. Answers will vary. Students may say that Claudius is aware that Hamlet knows the truth about how his father died, and so Claudius may be afraid that Hamlet will kill him, or that Claudius wants to send away this living reminder of his dead brother. Some students may point out that Claudius knows that the people of Denmark like Hamlet, and wants to send Hamlet away to shore up popular support for himself; that Claudius knows that Hamlet is trying to turn Gertrude against Claudius and break up the marriage; or that Claudius worries that word about the play will get out, and doesn't want Hamlet around to encourage the gossip.

62. Answers will vary.

63. One answer: Gallows-builders build stronger structures, since gallows last through thousands of inhabitants. Another answer: Gravediggers build the strongest structures of all, because theirs last until Judgment Day.

64. Shakespeare didn't fill *Hamlet* with clichéd quotes—the quotes originated in *Hamlet* and eventually became familiar. We only think of them as "quotes" because they've been woven into the English language. Phrases like "to be or not to be" are practically clichés to modern ears, but to audiences in Shakespeare's day, they were entirely fresh.

65. Answers will vary.

66. Answers will vary.

67. Answers will vary.

68. Translations should resemble this one:

Then I'll play the happy fool and let the laugh lines come with good humor. I'd rather overload my liver with wine than starve my heart by denying myself fun.

69. Translations should resemble this one:

There are some men whose faces never move or show any expression, like stagnant ponds covered in scum. They try to be serious on purpose so that people will think they're wise, important, and deep. It's as if they're saying, "I'm Sir Oracle, and when I start to talk, not even dogs should make noise!"

70. Answers will vary.

71. Answers will vary.

72. Antonio has insulted Shylock's money and business practices, which Shylock endured with "a patient shrug." Antonio has called Shylock a heathen and a "cutthroat dog." Now Antonio asks Shylock for a loan, and Shylock decides to remind Antonio of his insults, sarcastically inquiring how a dog like him (for so Antonio has called him) can be expected to lend money.

73. Translations should resemble this one:

If you don't repay me on the day we agree on, in the place we name, for the sum of money fixed in our contract, your penalty will be a pound of your pretty flesh, to be cut off and taken out of whatever part of your body I like.

74. Answers will vary.

75. By asking these questions, Shylock is suggesting that he is exactly like the Christians who treat him so badly. He has the same body as they do, the same passions and affections; he eats, gets injured and sick, feels the weather in the same way they do. At the end of the speech, Shylock suggests that he, like the Christians, should be allowed to seek revenge when it is appropriate.

76. Answers will vary.

77. The agreement specifies that Shylock can have a pound of flesh—but that's all. It doesn't say that he can have even a drop of blood, which he would undoubtedly draw if he tried to cut a pound out of Antonio.

78. Answers will vary.

79. Answers will vary.

80. Answers will vary.

81. Mowbray suggests that reputation is the most precious treasure anyone can possess. Without a spotless reputation, men are nothing more than dirt. Even if a man has wonderful qualities, if these qualities are hidden from other people, they might as well be buried away in a chest with ten locks. Honor is the same thing as life; thus, if honor is taken away, life is over. Mowbray lives for his honor and will die for it.

82. Translations should resemble this one:

> Men can be masters of their fate. It's not destiny's fault, but our own fault, that we're slaves.

83. Translations should resemble this one:

In front of the Capitol I met a lion who glared at me and skulked by without attacking me. And there were a hundred spooked women huddled together in fear who swore they saw men on fire walk up and down the street. And yesterday the night owl was hooting and shrieking in the marketplace at noon.

84. **Answers will vary.**

85. **In *Julius Caesar*, the phrase is pretty disgusting: the "dish fit for the gods" is Caesar's corpse. Today, we use the phrase to describe delicious meals.**

86. **Answers will vary.**

87. **Translations should resemble this one:**

Am I part of you only in a limited sense—I get to have dinner with you, sleep with you, and talk to you sometimes? Is my place on the outskirts of your happiness? If it's nothing more than that, then I'm your whore, not your wife.

88. **Answers will vary.**

89. **Answers will vary, but students should interpret Brutus's words to mean that he killed Caesar for the sake of Rome. Answers to the second question will vary.**

90. **Answers will vary, but possible words include *sarcastic*, *angry*, and *mocking*. Students might cite as evidence for their choice the repetition of the lines, "Yet Brutus says he was ambitious, / And Brutus is an honorable man." Students might also point out that "honorable" people don't usually commit murder.**

91. **Answers will vary.**

92. **Translations should resemble this one:**

Are you real? Are you a god, an angel, or a devil, that you make my blood turn cold and my hair stand on end? Tell me what you are.

93. **Antony insults Brutus and Cassius by comparing them to "apes," dogs, and servants. He also uses these similes to point out their hypocrisy. While they were pretending to lick Caesar's feet, as dogs would, and to bow to him, as servants would, they were really plotting to kill him.**

94. **Answers will vary.**

95. **Answers will vary.**

96. **Answers will vary.**

97. **Answers will vary.**

98. **Students may argue that Goneril's and Regan's answers are full of exaggerations, which suggests that they're not being completely honest. In contrast, it appears that Cordelia is speaking honestly—after all, she's risking losing part of a kingdom with her answer. Therefore, we can trust her when she says that she loves her father. Students may also argue that when Cordelia says she loves Lear as a daughter should love her father, she is really describing her love as powerful and strong. The mere fact that she does not use inflated language, as Goneril and Regan do, does not mean that she doesn't love him.**

99. **Translations should resemble this one:**

    I know you for what you really are, but as your sister I'm reluctant to name your faults. Love our father well.

100. **Translations should resemble this one:**

He was hotheaded even in the prime of his life. Now that he's old, we'll have to deal not only with his familiar character flaws, which have turned into deep-rooted habits, but also with the wild craziness that comes with old age.

101. Answers will vary.

102. Answers will vary.

103. Translations should resemble this one:

Listen up, uncle.
Have more than you show,
Speak less than you know,
Lend less than you owe,
Ride more than you walk,
Don't believe everything you hear,
Don't bet everything on one throw of the dice,
Leave your booze and your whore,
And stay indoors,
And you'll end up with more
Than two tens to a twenty.

104. Answers will vary.

105. Translations should resemble this one:

You useless bastard *Z*; you're as unnecessary as the letter *Z* is to the alphabet!

106. Answers will vary.

107. Answers will vary.

108. Answers will vary.

109. Answers will vary.

110. Answers will vary.

111. Answers will vary.

112. Answers will vary.

113. We use it much as Edmund does (though with no reference to fate) to mean that after a series of events, someone or something has arrived back where they started.

114. Translations should resemble this one:

> Don't forget the vows we made to each other. You have many chances to kill Albany. If you have the strength of will to do it, you'll have many opportunities. If he returns in triumph, then all is lost. I'll be his prisoner, and his bed will be my prison. Help me escape him, and you can take his place.
> Your—I wish I could say "wife"—loving servant, who is ready to love you, Goneril

115. Answers will vary.

116. Answers may include "what the devil," "what on earth, "what in the world," and "what in heaven's name."

117. First, he jokes that he's not sure he really fathered Hero. He says Hero's mother told him many times that Hero is his, but he suggests that she might have been lying. Leonato then jokes with Benedick, who asks him whether he doubted Hero's paternity. Leonato says he didn't doubt it, because Benedick was too young at that time to seduce Leonato's wife and father Hero.

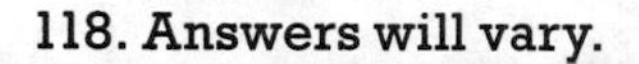

118. Answers will vary.

119. Benedick suggests that before Claudio fell in love, he was plainspoken; after he fell in love, he started talking in elaborate, flowery language. His speech is now like a banquet full of strange foods, as opposed to a more simple meal suitable for a soldier.

120. Answers will vary.

121. Translations should resemble this one:

CLAUDIO: She falls to her knees, weeps, sobs, beats her chest, tears her hair, prays, curses: "Oh, sweet Benedick! God give me patience!"

LEONATO: She really did, my daughter says so. Hero worries that Beatrice's emotions are so strong that she might hurt herself badly. It's really true.

122. Translations should resemble this one:

URSULA: But are you sure that Benedick loves Beatrice so much?

HERO: That's what the prince and my fiancé say.

URSULA: And did they ask you to tell Beatrice about this, madam?

HERO: They did want me to tell her, but I persuaded them that, if they truly loved Benedick, they would try to get him to battle his emotions and keep Beatrice in the dark.

123. When Hero says she has a heavy heart, meaning that she is sad, Margaret jokes that soon her chest will soon be heavier, because a man will be lying on top of her.

124. Answers will vary.

125. Answers will vary.

126. He sarcastically calls himself an ass; he then defines himself as a wise man, an officer, a handsome hunk of meat, someone who knows the law, a rich enough man, and a guy who used to have more money than he does now but nevertheless owns two robes and lots of lovely things.

127. Leonato means that it's easy to philosophize about ignoring pain when the pain is abstract, but all impressive theories about transcending suffering fly out the window when it's the philosopher himself who feels pain.

128. Dogberry acts as if he's reciting a long list of sins, when in fact he's just repeating the same offense (lying) over and over, in slightly different forms each time. Also, Dogberry misorders his list, saying "secondarily" when he's on the third item, "sixth and lastly" when he's on the fourth item and only halfway through the list, and "thirdly" when he's on the fifth item.

129. Answers will vary.

130. Answers will vary.

131. Pistol threatens to rob people, using violence if necessary, to get the money he needs.

132. Answers will vary but may include "kicked the bucket," "checked out," "met his maker," "passed away," "bought the farm," and "cashed in."

133. Answers will vary.

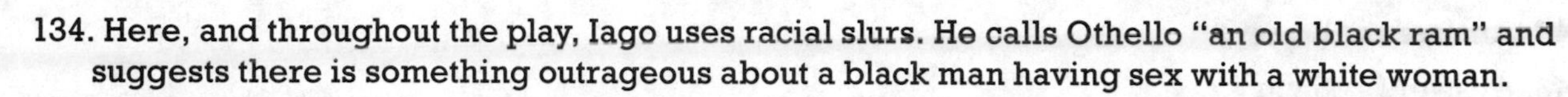

134. Here, and throughout the play, Iago uses racial slurs. He calls Othello "an old black ram" and suggests there is something outrageous about a black man having sex with a white woman.

135. Answers will vary.

136. She loved his stories of disasters, adventures, slavery, and close escapes from death. She loved him for the dangers he'd survived, and he loved her for pitying him.

137. Answers will vary.

138. Answers will vary.

139. Translations should resemble this one:

> Whoever steals my purse is stealing trash. It's something, it's nothing; it's yours, it's mine; and it has belonged to thousands of people. But he who steals my reputation robs me of something that doesn't make him richer and makes me poor indeed.

140. Answers will vary.

141. Although Iago claims that this dream proves nothing, really he wants Othello to believe it proves that Cassio has already slept with Desdemona.

142. Answers will vary.

143. Answers will vary.

144. Far from committing adultery, Desdemona is so pure and respectable that she can't even say the word *whore* in connection with herself. Her reluctance also suggests her unwillingness to believe that her husband has accused her of such monstrosities.

145. Answers will vary.

146. Answers will vary.

147. Answers will vary.

148. If Olivia is convinced that her brother is in heaven, as she says she is, there is no reason to mourn him, because he is in a lovely place.

149. Answers will vary.

150. Answers will vary.

151. Fabian suggests that Olivia only flirted with the boy because she wanted to make Sir Andrew jealous.

152. Answers will vary.

153. Answers will vary.

154. Answers will vary.

155. Richard isn't complaining about an unhappy time; rather, he's saying that the son of York (his brother) has turned things around, making a dark time light and turning winter into summer.

156. Answers will vary.

157. Answers will vary.

158. Answers will vary.

159. Romeo complains that Rosaline is wasting her beauty by not sleeping with anyone. She won't have children, and therefore her beauty won't be passed on to future generations.

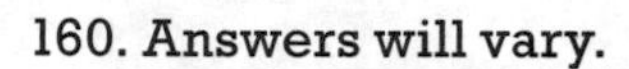

160. Answers will vary.

161. Romeo fears that whatever happens tonight will set in motion a chain of events that will lead to his own death. By referring to Romeo's death in the first act, Shakespeare is using **foreshadowing**—a device in which the author hints at what will happen later in the story.

162. Many readers assume that Juliet is asking *where* Romeo is. Actually, she is asking why he has to be Romeo—that is, why he has to be a member of the hated Montague family. The rest of her words relate to Romeo's family name. Juliet urges Romeo to give up his family and to "refuse" his name. She then decides that if he won't do that, she will give up her own name and cease being a Capulet.

163. Answers will vary.

164. Answers will vary.

165. Answers will vary.

166. Mercutio thinks that Benvolio is the kind of guy who goes into a bar, throws his sword on the table, and says, "I pray I never have to use you." But by the time he orders his second drink, he is pulling his sword on the bartender for no reason. In other words, Benvolio is the kind of guy who claims he's not violent but, in fact, flies off the handle all the time.

167. Translations should resemble this one:

> You can't talk about something you don't feel yourself. If you were as young as I am, if you were in love with Juliet, if you had just married her an hour ago, if you had murdered Tybalt, if you were lovesick like me, and if you were banished, then you might talk about it, then you might tear out your hair and fall to the ground, as I'm doing now. . . .

168. Answers will vary.

169. Translations should resemble this one:

> Capulet! Montague! See what a great evil results from your hate. Heaven has found a way to kill your joy with love.

170. Answers will vary, but students may say that the speaker is frustrated by the young man's refusal to have children. Since the young man will not have a "tender heir to bear his memory," his beauty will die when he does.

171. The speaker draws a distinction between love and sex. The speaker knows that the young man will sleep with women, but he (the speaker) thinks it is possible to continue loving the young man.

172. The speaker is having trouble explaining how much he loves his beloved. He compares himself to an actor who has forgotten his lines.

173. Answers will vary.

174. The sonnet suggests that writing about youth and beauty is the only way to preserve these qualities. If someone's good looks are captured in prose or poetry, which never ages, that person can live on forever in the pages of books.

175. The speaker claims that time has no effect on love. Although time may erase the youthful good looks of lovers, it won't erase their love for each other.

176. The speaker pretends to believe her, even though he knows "she lies," because he wants her to think of him as a young, innocent, "unlearnèd" man who doesn't understand the way the world works.
177. Answers will vary, but definitions should resemble the following definition from *Webster's* dictionary: "to expurgate, as a book, by omitting or modifying the parts considered offensive."
178. Answers will vary.
179. Answers will vary.
180. Answers will vary.

THE DAILY SPARK

Critical Thinking
Journal Writing
Poetry
Pre-Algebra
SAT: English Test Prep
Shakespeare
Spelling & Grammar
U.S. History
Vocabulary
Writing